SuperConsciousness
By
Practical Nada Yoga

Transcendence through Meditation
on the Subtle Inner Sounds

Rudra Shivananda

Alight Publications

2023

SuperConsciousness by Practical Nada Yoga

By Rudra Shivananda

First Edition Published in May 2023

Alight Publications
PO Box 277
Live Oak, CA 95953
http://www.alightbooks.com

Super-Consciousness by the Practice of Nada Yoga © 2022 by Runbir Singh.

All rights reserved. No part of this publication may be reproduced, stored in a retrieval system or database, or transmitted in any form or by any means electronic, mechanical, photocopying, recording, or otherwise without the prior written approval of the author or publisher.

Softback ISBN: 978-1-931833-64-6

Printed in the United States of America

Dedication

My deepest pranams to my Master
Yogiraj Gurunath Siddhanath
Who guides me to light, sound and
Beyond.

Table of Contents

Preface / 7

Introduction
What is Nada / 10
Om Pranava / 18
The Five-Body Existential Model / 21
A Simple Chakra Model / 24
The Subtle Sounds Come from Om / 28
The Manifestation of Sound / 29
The Universe and Nada / 31
The Center of Nada / 32
Spiritual Evolution / 33
Two Ways of Life / 40
Restoring Light and Harmony / 42
The Yogic Model of Higher Consciousness / 45
Benefits of Nada for Meditation / 56

The Practice of Nada Yoga
Time for Practice / 58
Precautions / 58
Guidelines for Practice / 59
Sequence for Nada Sadhana / 60
Asana Practice / 61

Breathing Exercise / 74
Brahmari Nada Pranayama / 81
Shanmukhi Mudra / 84
Manifestation of Nada / 88

Advanced Topics
Higher Consciousness - Samadhi / 92
Obstacles to Higher Consciousness and Remedies / 102
Nada in the Koshas / 109
Anahad and Anahat / 110
Nada Yoga and Gorakhnath / 111
The Ultimate Nada / 112
Nada and Turiya / 112

Appendix - Reference Texts
Yoga Taravali of Adi Shankaracharya / 116
Yoga Sikha Upanishad / 121

About Author / 130

Rudra Shivananda

Beyond the limits of mortal ears
Past the realms of sound we comprehend
Lies a symphony that we revere
That Song of infinite beauty without end

Preface

When I seriously started to search for a spiritual path in 1968, what struck me most was a common theme that ran through much of my readings. It was the veneration given to the mystical qualities of sound and vibrations, particularly the sound called "OM" in its various forms.

Strange to say, it would be over 20 years later that I would begin to experience and appreciate these mystical sounds, as my journey took me through the meandering streams of different spiritual traditions. It was only then that I finally came home to the practice of Kriya Yoga, the epitome of the fusion of Hatha and Raja yogas bestowed to humanity by Mahavatar Babaji through his disciple Lahiri Mahasaya. In the course of my practice, I was able to experience the various mystical sounds that had intrigued me in the past.

It was a satisfying surprise that spurred me to investigate more deeply my passion for light, sound and vibration which led me to the age-old but not well-known path of Nada Yoga or as it has been known since pre-history, Nada Anusandhana.

It was quickly apparent after a little research that Nada Yoga techniques have been incorporated into many of the newer yoga systems. After peeling the layers, and discovering the source, it seemed appropriate to share the theory and practice of this extremely effective yogic tradition with my brothers and sisters in the spiritual community.

We are assured by the great sages that this form of yoga leads ultimately to Self-realization and to Cosmic Consciousness. The process and techniques are based on the text of the Nath tradition called the Hatha Pradipika. The model of the higher consciousness used is from the Yoga Patanjal (Yoga Sutras of Patanjali).

In the Appendix, I've included two texts which are less well-known than the Hatha Pradipika, but have been helpful in my understanding of Nada Yoga. They are the Yoga Taravali and the Yoga Sikha Upanishad.

Let me hasten to clarify that a book is not a substitute for personal instruction from a qualified acharya or spiritual teacher, but can serve as an introduction and useful reference. In the course of my practice and studies, I've not come across a thorough exposition of Nada Yoga. May this small token in some measure serve as an offering to the grace of the Masters who have imparted these ancient teachings.

Introduction

What is Nada Yoga?

When a spiritual practitioner's subtle body becomes purified and there is a withdrawal of the senses from the external environment towards the internal center, she will experience various inner sounds. These should not be confused with the physical sounds of the body resulting from the rushing of blood or contraction of various organs. These inner sounds can lead to higher consciousness.

Many seekers have mistakenly been bothered by hearing a persistent "noise" in their ears and have sought medical help to get rid of this nuisance! The medical profession cannot explain what it is but gives it a name – tinnitus, without even being able to provide any real meaningful treatment. It is claimed to have multiple causes and a variety of helpful suppression devices are prescribed. A whole industry has grown up around helping those afflicted with this mysterious illness. However, in the majority of instances, it is neither a physical or psychological ailment but the expression of the cosmic sound vibration within our consciousness. There may be rare instances where it is really an illness, but it is rare indeed.

Those who are suffering from this malady would do well to consider refining their body-mind complex to attune to the sounds instead of partaking of harmful drugs. The sounds may be a clarion call to take up meditation.

The true inner sounds are called anahata or "unstruck" or uncaused to differentiate them from normal sounds or even higher vibrations which are caused by the effect of one physical object striking against another physical object. That inner sound that the yogis listen to is called nada or the divine flow. We can experience this nada as a flute sound, a roaring river or thunder, sound of crickets or electricity as well as other variations such as spontaneous sounds that can be interpreted in human language. Nada can have many degrees of manifestation depending on the level that is accessed.

At the cosmic level, nada is called para [that is, para-nada] and it is to this level that aspiring seekers hope to reach. This plane of existence is called the causal plane. At the next lower level nada is called pashyanti - it is a mental vibration that corresponds to the mental plane. This is followed by the nada of the madhyama, that is a whispering or mental recitation, vibrating from the astral worlds. Finally, nada takes on the gross form of the spoken word in the physical world.

As the yogis followed this nada to its ultimate point or bindu, they experienced the state of Shiva-Shakti or pure consciousness vibrating with energy, a state that transcended time and space. From their shared experience, these yogis formulated their evolutionary model in which nada is the first evolute to emerge from Shiva-Shakti and bindu is the nucleus that holds this vibration.

Nada Yoga is the system of concentration which increases awareness to the subtle manifestation of this divine vibration which can be "heard" internally without our intentional making of a sound whether aloud, in a whisper of even mentally. The aim of Nada Yoga is to reach the para-nada and achieve the highest consciousness expressed as sound called Shabdabrahman – the Divine Sound.

The authority for Nada Yoga goes back to antiquity, to the most revered spiritual texts called the Upanishads. There are 108 recognized Upanishads, some dating back to 1000 BCE. The Nada-Bindu Upanishad gives a thorough foundation for the system of Nada:

> Seated in the yogic perfect pose
> With aid of Vaishnavi-mudra practice
> Be absorbed in the inner sound from the right ear
> (Verse 31)

To the modern spiritual practitioner, it may appear that Nada Yoga doesn't seem to be mentioned much and its lineage vanished. However, the truth is that it has been incorporated and absorbed into most of the modern spiritual yoga lineages and forms the basis of a few modern groups under different labels.

The practice variously called jyoti-mudra, shambavi mudra or yoni mudra plays an important role in Kriya, Tantra, Hatha, Laya, Kundalini and Shabda yogas, as well as in the lineages of the Kabir Panth and Radhasoamis.

Consider a quote from the 8th century spiritual giant Shankaracharya: 'With a calm mind and abandoning all thoughts, meditate upon Nada if you desire to attain perfection in Yoga.' Or one from the Shiva Samhita, a Hatha Yoga treatise: 'The best posture is the perfect pose, the best way to cultivate strength is by holding of breath, the best energetic seal is the

Kechari Mudra, and the best way to dissolve the mind is by Nada."

There is a basic difference in polarity between Mantra and Nada, although eventually, they lead to the same point. In mantra, the practitioner repeats a set of sounds that have the power to calm the mind and lead to higher consciousness. In Nada, there is a mode of listening and being absorbed in the inner, "unstruck sounds", a witnessing and detachment from all mental processes. In Mantra yoga, in the active repetition of the mantra, there is also a process of becoming passively absorbed in its vibration. Therefore, in reality, both are active-passive but from different poles.

In Nada, we see the vibration of light – the bindu point, before becoming absorbed in the para-nada of cosmic consciousness. This is an important part of the practice of Kriya Yoga.

There is a close connection between the evolutionary yogic techniques of Kriya Yoga and the little known system of spiritual development called Nada Yoga. In the Kriya system, there are a series of techniques called Omkar Kriyas which involve listening to the sound vibrations of Om. Also, an advanced technique called Jyoti Mudra which requires both the vibrations of light and sound. These parts of Kriya Yoga are an integration of the light sound techniques of Nada Yoga.

The techniques of Kriya Yoga are normally only transmitted by authorized acharyas or spiritual preceptors in person and so it is not possible to use them to illustrate or compare to the Nada Yoga techniques.

The most widely documented and accesible system of yoga is that of Hatha Yoga. There is a popular misconception that this is a health and exercise system. It is in fact, a yogic system for purifying the subtle body of a spiritual practitioner in order for the practice to go into deeper and higher states of consciousness.

The principal text for this system is called Hatha (Yoga) Pradipika and a large portion of the last chapter is in fact about Nada Yoga:

> Now I begin to describe the practice of nada that has been given out by Gorakshanantha and which has been accepted even by those unable to realize truth or have not studied the scriptures. Of all the myriad ways for attaining dissolution of the mind and senses given by Lord Shiva, the practice of Nada is the best.
> (Verses 4.65-66)

We shall be referring to the HYP [Hatha Yoga Pradipika] often when we are learning the actual practices of Nada Yoga.

Another major spiritual system that provides much guidance in the unstruck sound is that of Tantra Yoga. One of the key texts that provide a large number of tantric techniques is the Shri Vijnana Bhairava Tantra, sometimes called the Book of Secrets. In it, there are several suggestions on how to listen to the inner sounds to attain to different levels of awareness - which type of sound and where to listen to it:

> One who is adept in listening to the unstruck sound

> like a continuous rushing river in the heart center
> attains the supreme state of Brahama by mastery
> of Shabdabrahman [the Divine Sound]
> (verse 38)

The inner sounds can sometimes appear to the seeking mind as different types of musical instruments for the different seekers but the final objective is the same provided that there is full concentration:

> When one-pointed awareness on the prolonged inner sound
> of different musical instruments, such as stringed,
> wind and percussion, is gradually established,
> the body becomes the supreme space
> (verse 41)

Although the devotional schools of spirituality do not give much importance to yogic practices, they are actually a development of the yoga of devotion called Bhakti Yoga. Most of these schools eventually become religious in the growth. However, if we examine some of the writings of their scriptures and founders, we can find that Nada is a key aspect of their spiritual experience and insight.

They call the unstruck sound Nam [name of God] or Shabda. This Nam is of two kinds - the first is utterable and given by the spiritual Master or scripture for repetition. The second is unutterable - the unstruck sound, the logos, the Word, the celestial music which vibrate within everyone as Nada. It is by the practice of the repetition of the utterable Nam, the true unspoken Nam is contacted, the taste of which is bliss.

Let us consider the words of Guru Gobind Singh [10th Guru of the Sikh Dharma] in his Shabad Hazare:

> Your self-control whould be the one-stringed instrument
> And the Name of the Lord your alms.
> When the supreme note of his Name resound,
> The unstruck melody will form

Guru Nanak, the founder and 1st Guru of the Sikh Dharma exhorted his followers to meditate on the Name of God to attain to divine bliss with the Nada resounding in their minds:

> Those engrossed in meditating on His Name,
> Is protected in all His mercy
> He in whose heart He abides,
> Meeting Him is untold bliss

> Don't waste time - Meditate on Him.
> He is the Master who provdes forever.
> The devotee who perfectly remembers the Lord,
> The unstruck melody resound in his mind.

What then is this utterable name of God, or Nam? Every religion seems to have different names for their deities and aren't there thousands if not tens of thousands of names of gods in the Hindu Dharma? In spite of differences, the common Name over the course of human evolution has been distilled to Om or Onkkar or Amen etc. We shall examine this in more detail in a subsequent section.

At the heart of many types of yoga, the awakening and raising of a mysterious latent power called Kundalini is necessary to accomplish the goal of attaining superconscious states or samadhi. A spiritual adept of the Kashmiri tantric school has described this nadavedha type of rising Kundalini:

> For him, the rise of prana kundalini begins with
> the blissful force of breath touching the
> muladhara chakra, which then begins to move.
> Simultaneously the blissful force is transformed into Nada.
> This sensation of nada continues as prana kundalin rises
> to penetrate the navel, then the heart,
> then the throat and finally the eyebrows.
> (Swami Lakshmanjoo)

OM Pranava

Since time immemorial, the ancient sages have transmitted OM as the closest approximation to the creative matrix.

It is called the "unstruck" sound because it is not produced by any mechanical means and is not propelled through space, but is the fundamental Omnipresent vibration, called the "music of the spheres" by the Pythagorians. It is the Amen of the Christians.

When properly charged with life-force, sound is the most powerful principle that can bring about all manifestations. Sound is the first manifestation of the Absolute. The Divine Will to create caused a vibration, which eventually became the primordial Sound, and that Sound is OM, from which the rest of the Universe manifested. OM is the basis for all creation, and should it one day cease to Sound, the Universe will be re-absorbed back into the Divine.

Similarly, from the principle that "As the macrocosm, so the microcosm", our bodies and mind all have the Sound of OM as the foundation. In order to reach our True Self, we need to re-discover the healing Sound of OM within ourselves. The Sound of OM naturally forms the basis of the seven chakras or Energy Centers in our individual manifestation. Each chakra is able to work with a different harmonic of OM, with the 1st Center sounding at the lowest harmonic, while the 7th Center sounds at the highest harmonic. We will be studying the subtle body chakras in more detail in a subsequent section.

To understand the power of Sound, we only have to see how music, which is one of its physical manifestations, affects animals, and how human beings are soothed or agitated by music. Scientific experiments with beds of sand have shown a particular sound will form a definite and specific shape, and different sounds form different shapes.

OM is the manifest representation of Divinity and the Universe of Creation. It is the primal sound from which the universe evolved. The chanting of OM quickly relaxes the mind and body, generating spiritual power and accelerating evolutionary transformation.

The sound of OM is composed of the combination of the vowel sounds of A and U, with the letter M, and the sound of silence. Innumerable correspondences have been created by the ancients for the four parts of OM : A represents the physical world and wakeful state, U represents the Astral world and dream state, M the causal world and deep sleep state, while the silence represents the spiritual world.

The form of OM is shown in [**Figure 1**], consisting of three curves, one semicircle and a dot. The bottom curve denotes the wakeful state, the upper curve the deep sleep, and the curve in between signifies the dream state. The dot represents the Absolute state of Super-consciousness while the surrounding semicircle represents the conditional world of conventional reality.

The complete syllable OM is considered by the sages to be the highest knowable reality, and those who know it are said to attain all their desires – it is the source of everything and nothing. The ancients have said that by uttering OM as one departs the body at death, liberation from the cycle of rebirth will be attained.

Figure 1 : Om

The Five-Body Existential Model

In order to understand how NadaYoga works and its process, we need to learn more about our subtle nature consisting of a series of subtle bodies that give expression to our phenomenal being and the energetic centers within our subtle bodies which are responsible for our physical, energetic, emotional and mental nature.

Refer to Figure 2.

1. The physical body is what most of us identify with. It is the only reality which the majority of humanity recognizes, being composed of blood and bones, the nervous system and sense organs

2. The energy body is just above our normal conscious perception, but can be sensed in recognition of the presence of vitality. It is like an overlay on the physical body energizing and regulating the physical cells. It acts as a channel between the physical world and the higher subtle worlds. Here is where the chakras or energy centers are particularly active.

3. The emotional body serves as the mediation between the physical and mental bodies, converting the physical vibrations from the neutral sensations into the "emotionally charged sensations" by adding the qualities of "pleasant" or "unpleasant" or encapsulating it with feelings such as desire or fear. Most physical diseases arise from the emotional or energy bodies.

4. The mental body is the abode of knowledge and analytical thinking. The "emotionally charged sensations" from the emotional body is processed into perceptual units and fitted into patterns calling forth responses which vibrate back through the emotional body back into the physical realm, causing a physical reaction. This is the realm of thoughts and habit patterns.

5. The causal body is both the home of wisdom and of our karmic debts. This is the abode of the evolving soul. Higher abstract and intuitive insights arise from here.

The five-body complex exists and functions in different "dimensions" and each is maintained by a different type of energy, from the physical chemical reactions to the subtlest consciousness energy. Each of the bodies has its own energy centers or chakras as well as energy channels for controlling and distributing its own level of energy. Orthodox science only recognizes the centers and channels associated with the physical body, where the cardio-vascular system represents the channels, and the brain and various nerve plexuses correspond to the energy centers. As the chakras are activated and awakened, you will become aware of the corresponding dimension of reality, giving you a fuller understanding of the higher dimensions.

During the process of Nada Yoga, the various chakras in the subtle bodies are awakened and give rise to a variety of subtle vibrations which are heard during meditation.

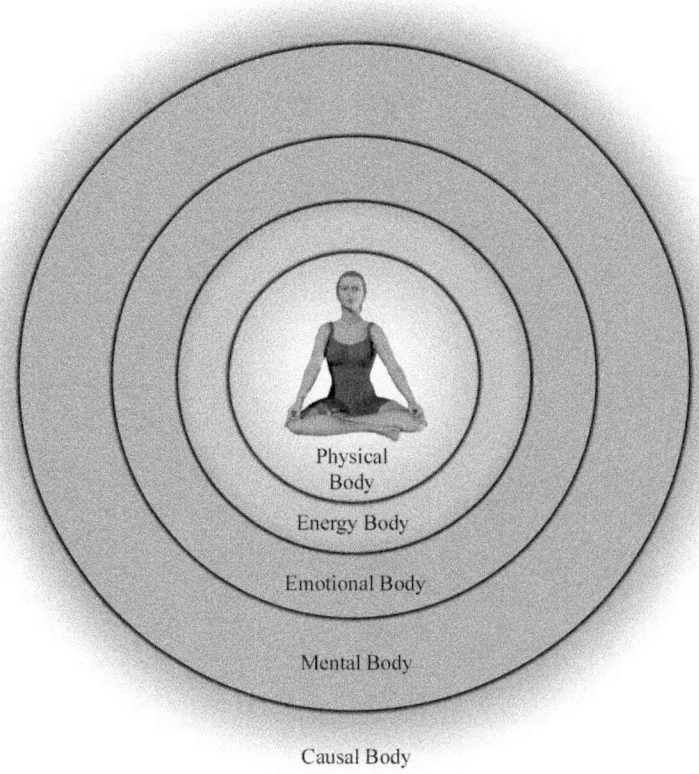

Figure 2 : Five Body Model

A Simple Chakra Model

It has been pointed out in ancient yogic texts, that yogis are those who truly know the Chakras or Energy Centers. This exemplifies how critical and potentially complex this whole topic can become. Each chakra vibrates to particular frequencies and can be activated by external sounds and words such as during mantra practice. For the practice of Nada Yoga, we are listening for the vibrations – rather than using mantras to vibrate them, the process is by purifying the subtle channels and bodies.

These Energy Centers cannot be found by dissecting the physical body, but only through achieving higher states of consciousness. Figure 3 gives the location of the chakras in relation to the physical body. They are called wheels because of the circular movement of the energies that whirl in an out of them. They are balls of light, and you will be able to feel their circular movement as you progress in your spiritual evolution.

These Energy Centers are affected by changes in our internal states, as well as by external vibrations, such as thoughts, words, or actions of others. In the average person, these Centers are functioning sub-optimally, and are not harmonized with each other. As the health of the person is decreased through pollution and tension, the more out of tune these Centers become. We need to harmonize these imbalanced Energy Centers in order to progress in our Nada Yoga practice.

Center 1: This is also called the muladhara chakra (root center), and is located at the base of the spine in the perineum and is the root and support of all the other centers. It is connected with the subtle element "earth" representing solidity, and therefore is closely related to the physical body.

Center 2: This is located two inches above the 1st Center along the spine and is called svadhisthana chakra. It is associated with the subtle element water, representing fluidity and movement. This is the center for the emotional body.

Center 3: This is located at the level of the navel, and is associated with the subtle element fire, representing transformation of energy. It is called manipura chakra and is closely related to the energy body.

Center 4: This is located at the spine at the heart level and is associated with the subtle element air, representing the mind. It is called anahata chakra and is the center of the mental body.

Center 5: This is located at the throat and is associated with the subtle element ether, representing consciousness. This is the center for the causal or spiritual body. It is called vishuddhi chakra and is considered the seat of the soul.

Center 6: This is located in the center of the head at the level just above the eyes. It is traditionally called the "third eye" or ajna chakra and is the center for super-consciousness.

Center 7: this is located at the crown of the head and is associated with the Absolute or Transcendent Reality. It is called sahasrara chakra or the thousand-petal lotus.

When the first six chakras are tuned and balanced and finally, fully awakened, they will open our consciousness to the Divine Reality of the seventh Center. During this process, the following sounds or some form of them are heard:

Chakra	Sound
Muladhara chakra	bumble bee
Svadhisthana chakra	flute
Manipura chakra	harp
Anahata chakra	bell
Vishuddhi chakra	sea roar
Ajna chakra	thunder

There are different descriptions of the sounds because it is a subjective experience and we are trying to classify the sounds according to our preconceptions. It is best to keep an open mind and try to experience whatever comes.

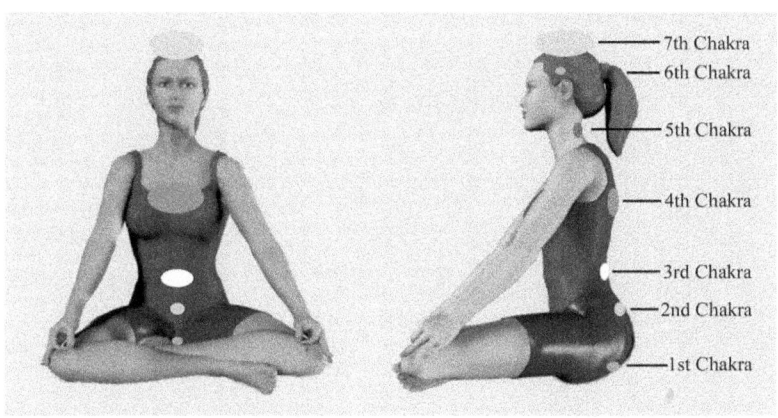

Figure 3 : The Chakra Model

The Subtle Sounds Come From Om

Where do the nada sounds come from? The mystic OM does not have a translation. It is called the "birthing hum of the universe", since according to the sages, every atom and being in the universe is vibrating with some harmonic of this sound. It is the sound that gave birth to the universe – what is called "The Word of God." In the scriptures of ancient India, OM is considered as the most powerful of all the mantras. The others are considered aspects of OM, and OM is the matrika (mother) of all other mantras. The syllable OM is quite familiar to Indians, since it occurs in every prayer. Invocation to most gods begins with this syllable OM which is also pronounced as AUM. The syllable OM is not specific to Indian culture. It has religious significance in other religions also. OM is not given any specific definition and is considered to be a cosmic sound, a primordial sound and even the totality of all sounds. In the West, this Indian tradition of beginning all names of the Divine with Om seems to have a counterpart in the use of the words that describe God – Omnipresent, Omnipotent or Omniscience. It is amen and amin, as well as the alpha and the omega.

Scientific studies have shown that chanting OM resulted in significant brain wave frequency changes, as evidenced in the subject's EEG readings. Gujare, Ladhake, and Thakare from Spina's college of Engineering & Technology in Maharashtra, India, explain the reading in this way, "From this we could conclude that chanting OM mantra results in stabilization of

[the] brain, removal of worldly thoughts and an increase of energy. It means that concentrating on OM mantra and continuously doing it slowly shifts our attention. It is a reflection of the most fundamental interlocking processes in our bodies...the harmony we play echoes the harmonic relationships of every vital system i.e. our heartbeat, our breathing, our brainwaves pulsing, our neuronal firing, our cells throbbing, our metabolic, enzymatic, and hormonal rhythms and our behaviors in our addictions and our habits. In this sense OM mantra is a brain stabilizer, by practicing it one can enter deeper and deeper into a natural state, which is also an energy medicine for human beings under stress."

During the practice of Nada Yoga, we are tuning in to various aspects of this universal vibration called Om. The process of unfolding from our current vibratory state to that of the nada is one that is likened to that of evolution – of spiritual evolution.

The Manifestation of Sound

There are four stages of manifestation of sound according to frequency and subtlety or grossness. The four stages are: (i) para, (ii) pashyanti, (iii) madhyama and (iv) vaikhari. These four stages of sound should be understood scientifically. We are not concerned with sounds that are audible whether through our sense organ or through instruments. Only the transcendental 'sound' is the vehicle that can go beyond the mind.

Para means 'transcendental, 'beyond' or 'the other side'. It is beyond the reach of the indriyas, or sense organs, and the mind and other means of cognition. Hence para nada is the transcendental sound. It is indicative of a truth that there is a sphere of super-consciousness where the sound is heard in different dimensions.

Para or transcendental sound has the highest vibration frequency. This intense vibration faculty makes para inaudible. Various texts mention that para sound has no vibration. It is a sound that has no movement and therefore no frequency. It is a still sound, but we cannot conceive of a sound that has no vibration, no movements, no motion. When a sound goes to its maximum pitch, it attains a sudden stillness, and that is para nada.

In the Upanishads, the sound of Om is said to be the manifestation of para. The audible chant of Om which we produce is not para because it is physical, subject to our hearing, understanding and logic. Therefore, the audible Om cannot be called the transcendental Om. Para is a cosmic and transcendental sound devoid of all movement. It is both still and infinite. It has shape and light too. Its nature is jyoti (light). It is different from all sounds usually heard or conceived. The Upanishads clearly state, "That is Om, that sound is Om."

The Universe and Nada

According to nada yogis and the scriptures dealing with the subject of nada yoga, the nada brahma, or the ultimate and transcendental sound, is the seed from which the entire creation has evolved. A nada yogi believes that the world is but a projection of sound alone. The whole macro cosmic universe is a projection of sound vibrations. From that sound the whole world has evolved. In the Bible there is the reference: "In the beginning was the word, and the word was with God." This word is called the nada or the shabda. Sufis in India call it surat. Surat or shabda yoga is another name for nada yoga practice. The Sufi saints of philosophical temperament also believe that out of sound and form the world evolved. The nada yogis believe that the five elements, five karmendriyas, five jnanendriyas, the fourfold mind and the three gunas have evolved out of one eternal sound. It means that prakriti, the material, mental, psychic and intellectual universe, is all an outcome of nada brahma. This is the ultimate belief of all nada yogis. So a nada yogi believes in a reality which has manifested itself in the form of vibration. It is a vibration that either does not vibrate at all or at such a high frequency that it is beyond the reach of the human faculty.

The eternal or original nada has the highest rate of frequency and vibration. When any object vibrates at a tremendous and unimaginable speed, it becomes still. It means that the highest point of motion and vibration is stillness. And that nada appears to be the creative principle of all matter and the entire material substance.

Nada yogis contend that everything in the universe originated and evolved from the eternal and infinite nada. In this context a study of the Upanishads is recommended, with special reference to Nada Bindu Upanishad and Hamsopanishad.

Music is also a materialized form of nada and the movements of prana in the body are also nothing but the expressions of nada. The purpose of nada yoga sadhana is to find out the primal, the finest, the ultimate inner sound - the word or shabda. In order to discover this transcendental and non-empirical sound, the process starts from the external gross sound. From there the ultimate form of sound is conceivable only through going into the deeper realms of our consciousness.

The Center of Nada

There are different centers where the transcendental nada is said to be situated. Bhaktas try to find the centre of their ishta in anahata (their inner Divinity in the heart center). Yogis try to find the centre of intuition in ajna (the third-eye center). Vedantins try to find the center of hiranyagarbha in sahasrara or the crown chakra.

Likewise, nada yogis locate the center of nada in bindu. Bindu is the center where the continuous, eternal, inaudible, unbroken and unbeaten sound goes on. For the purpose of the discovery of nada, it is true that the bindu has to be discovered primarily and finally.

Before venturing into the depth of this science, it would be better for the aspirant to locate or discover the mental, astral and psychic nature of the sound of nada. Different nada yoga practices are introduced in order to help the aspirant to get through the different psychic and non-physical sounds, before the consciousness can finally be attuned with the real nada.

Spiritual Evolution

We've often heard from saints and read from books that each of us is potentially Divine. What does this mean when most of us certainly don't feel or behave in a divine manner or have the powers of divinity in our imagination? My Master SatGurunath would often say to us that "we are divine to the extant that we know divinity". It seems like that we have the potential to be divine but something more is needed to put us to that state. Realizing our divinity is not simply an intellectual understanding but a thorough upgrade of our body, mind and soul and that is what we call spiritual evolution.

Reality as perceived by the sages is very glorious – we are each one of us star-seed. The earth itself is but stardust, born from stellar debris, and is constantly evolving. From the earth we obtain our bodies, and from our star, the Sun, we receive our life, our soul.

There is an impetus in earth matter to evolve. The physical aspects of evolution have been established by Darwin. Few dispute the evolution from single cell toward multi-cell organisms, from invertebrate to vertebrate, from reptiles to mammals. It is a helpful analogy to the immensity that is spiritual evolution, the evolution of consciousness. The ancient masters of yoga have always recognized and taught evolution. In fact, the goal of these ancient spiritual scientists was to accelerate the evolutionary process.

Figure 4 shows the state of a "normal human" being limited to body and superficial mental consciousness, and yet controlled by the vaster unknown depths of the sub-conscious and unconscious. This is the mode where we suffer from the limitations of the five senses as well as our own hidden karmic tendencies buried beyond our conscious grasp. Science has proven what the ancient seers taught, that human beings are living with an incomplete picture of reality. In fact, our senses give us a very small glimpse of the material universe and hardly anything of the sublte.

Based on the teachings of the sages, we can formulate a more comprehensive model of our our existential reality. Figure 5 shows how the "individual" body/mental consciousness is only one mode of a vaster framework of evolution to soul consciousness, universal consciousness and finally to naked and empty Being, from which all beings arise. The model is helpul from the perspective of evolution of consciousness.

When human evolution advances to the highest level, the subconscious mind is cleared, ego is dissolved and super-consciousness is awakened. Even more than ordinary human consciousness is light-years beyond animal consciousness, so super-consciousness is beyond the ordinary human intellect, logic and reasoning. Figure 6 shows the relationship of spiritual evolution and physical evolution. It shows how humanity has evolved beyond the animal instincts to achieve ego consciouness. The challenge now is to evolve beyond to superconsciousness and eventually to uneversal consciousness.

When the highest level of evolution is not only isolated among a few exceptional individuals, but is prevalent in a society, then that society exists completely in harmony with Nature, beyond technology, religion and violence.

The energy centers are also related to the corresponding centers of consciousness, as shown by Figure 7, and the self-healing modalities for the chakras will have a positive evolutionary effect on consciousness, as well. It is precisely because of the interconnectedness of gross matter, subtle matter and consciousness that we can utilize our physical body and mind to evolve our consciousness.

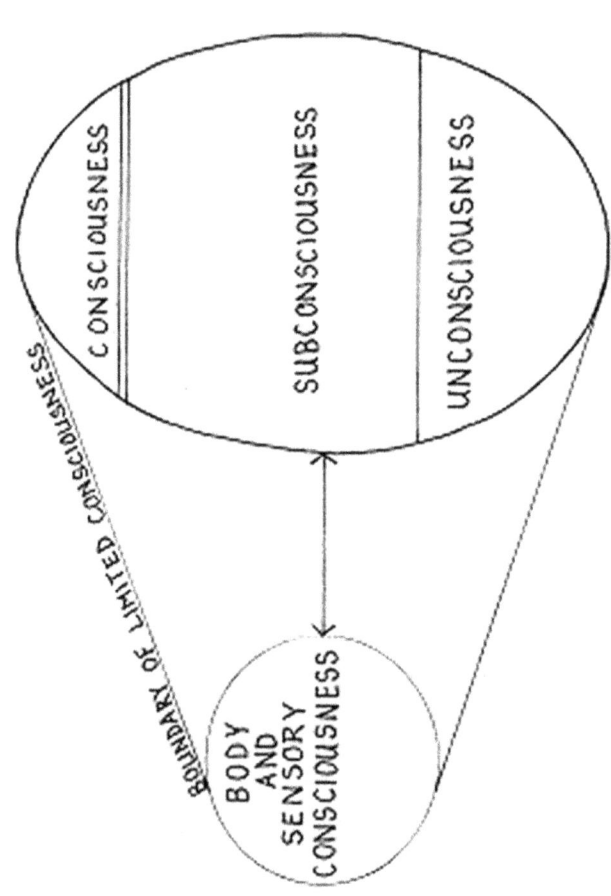

Figure 4: Limited Consciousness

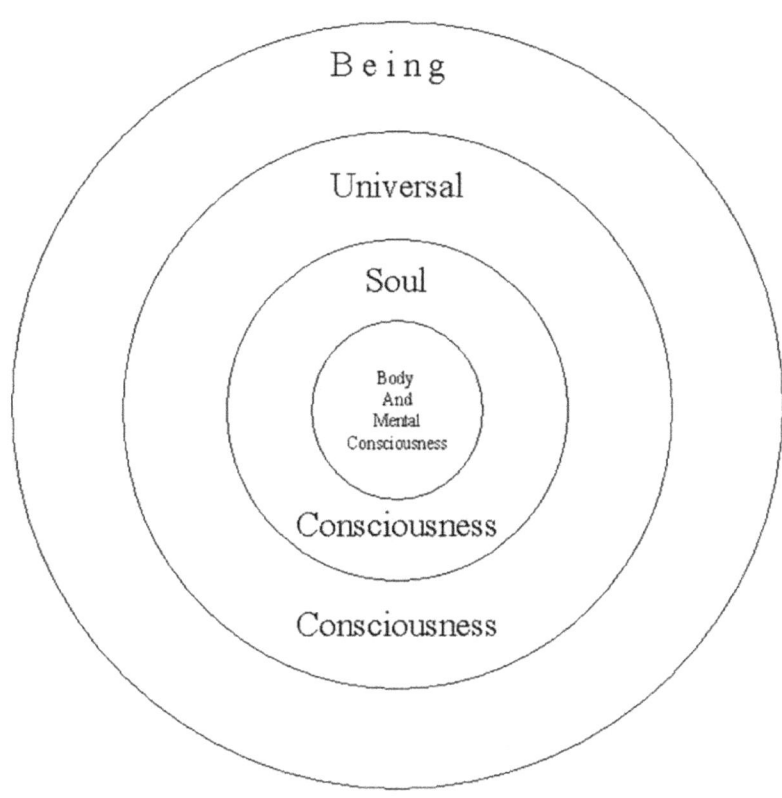

Figure 5: Evolution of Consciousness

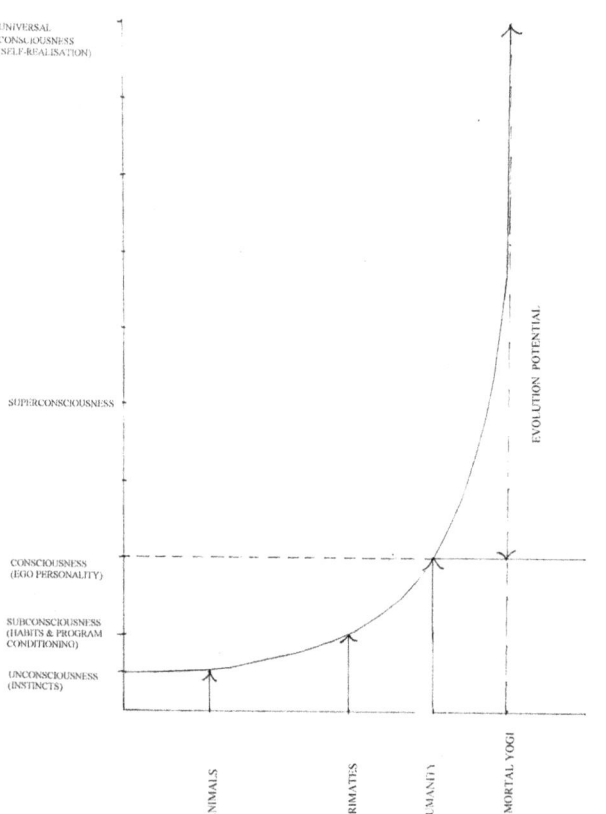

Figure 6: Evolution of Body and Consciousness

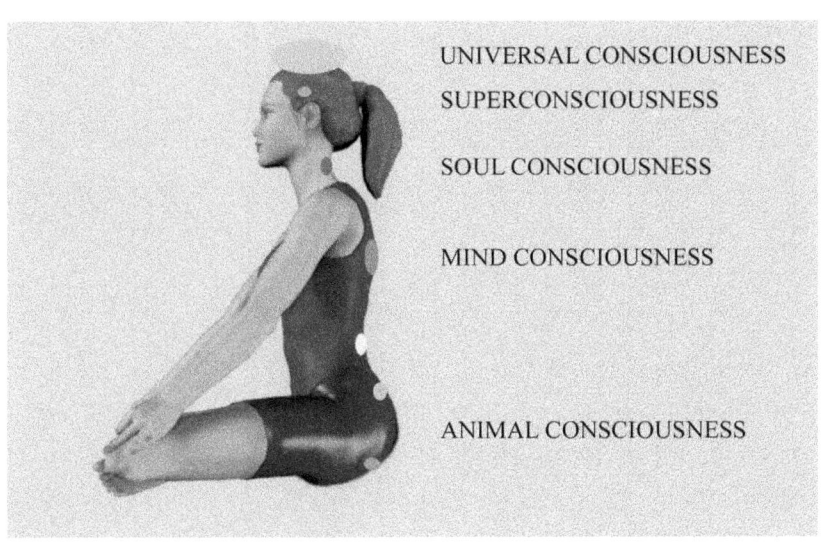

Figure 7 :
Levels of Consciousness with Energy Centers

Two Ways of Life – downward and upward paths

Pravritti means to live amidst worldly duties and interests with the senses and actions directed primarily towards the external world.

Nivritti, on the other hand, is the path of "turning back", the path of turning within towards spiritual contemplation, and placing the Divine at the center of our existence after fulfilling our familial and professional duties.

For as long as we live in Pravritti our thoughts turn mainly towards worldly things – to pleasure and hobbies and worrying about fame, position and possessions. Initially school and education occupy our thoughts, then later profession and family. Finally, in old age we worry about our health and our progeny.

Of course, based on tradition, it is proper and necessary for us to fulfill our responsibilities and duties to our family and society - there is a no problem with being comfortable or prosperous. However, if one cares about nothing else and is totally wrapped up in these temporary things, constantly grasping after them, believing that it is absolutely essential to "make or do" something, then their energies are wasted outwardly.

When we strive after possessions and are never satisfied, then it is a sign that we are still on the downward path of pravritti. What is the goal of life? The sages teach that it is an error to think that the goal in life is to experience and enjoy the world only in a sensory manner. What does enjoyment mean? A wise person knows that desires are never-ending. We are constantly hungry and thirsty, even if we have just eaten well. No worldly pleasures satisfy us forever. Desire soon rises anew. Only something long lasting and unchanging is able to give us true satisfaction. That which changes is unreal – only the eternal and unchanging Self is real.

If we follow one path we will inevitably reach where that path leads. When we turn our mind too much towards the outer world we lose contact with our inner world and to Divinity. Therefore the only way out of the illusion that the material world is all there is (Maya) is through nivritti.

As we keep the mind free of worldly desires and turn towards the Divine, the attitude of nivritti should predominate, not just externally but more importantly inwardly. Neither money nor possessions make us inwardly rich - rather, true wealth lies in a peaceful heart and contentment. Only in nivritti can the soul permanently quench its thirst for happiness and knowledge.

One day, no matter how many life-cycles it takes, every human will attain perfection. The two ways of life are like two branches of a tree. The pravritti branch bends down towards the world, whereas the nivritti branch goes upwards towards divine consciousness. We will traverse both paths – when we tire of pravritti, then we will begin the nivritti cycle.

Restoring Light and Harmony

In yogic philosophy, all matter in the universe arises from the fundamental substrate called prakriti. From prakriti arises the three primary gunas or qualities that create the essential aspects of all nature—energy, matter and consciousness. These three gunas are tamas (darkness), rajas (activity), and sattva (lightness). All three gunas are always present in all beings and objects but vary in their relative amounts leading to various levels of material attachment and delusion.

Lord Krishna has said (BG 14:05 – 14:08):

> The eternal embodied soul to the material body bound
>   The three-fold principle binding mind is found
>
>   Pure and good, illuminating sattva snare
> Attachment to happiness and knowledge beware
>
> Restless and passionate, intense selfish rajas craving
> Attachment to desire borne on fruits of work saving
>
> Ignorant and lazy, tamas delusion inducing wrap
> Attachment to negligence and non-action soul trap

Understanding the gunas is critical to knowledge of human psychology. The mind is highly unstable and fluctuates under the changing dominance of the different gunas. The temporarily dominant guna acts like a lens that effects our perceptions and perspective of the world. For example, when the mind is dominated by rajas it will experience world events as chaotic activity and it will react in a passionate and restless manner.

Yoga teaches that we have the ability to consciously alter the levels of the gunas in our bodies and minds. The gunas cannot be separated or removed in oneself, but can be consciously acted upon to encourage their increase or decrease. A guna can be increased or decreased through the interaction and influence of external objects, lifestyle practices and thoughts. An important way to regulate these gunas in body and mind is through ayurvedic cooking which seeks to increase the sattvic, decrease rajasic and avoid the tamasic foods.

Sattvic foods are fresh, juicy, light, nourishing, sweet and tasty and give the necessary energy to the body without taxing it. It is the foundation of higher states of consciousness. Examples are juicy fruits, fresh vegetables that are easily digestible, fresh milk and butter, whole soaked or sprouted beans, grains and nuts, many herbs and spices in the right combinations with other foods.

Rajasic foods are bitter, sour, salty, pungent, hot and dry. They increase the speed and excitation of the nervous system and chaotic thoughts in the mind. It is the foundation of motion, activity and pain. Examples are sattvic foods that have been overcooked or oil-fried, foods and spices that are strongly exciting such as garlic and onions.

Tamasic foods are dry, old and decaying. They consume large amounts of energy while being digested. They are the foundation of ignorance, doubt, pessimism. Examples are foods that have been strongly processed, canned or frozen and/or are old, stale or incompatible with each other – meat is especially tamasic.

Saints and seers can survive easily on sattvic foods alone but householders living in the world also need rajasic energy to keep pace with its changes. It is necessary to keep a balance as much as possible.

Since all gunas create attachment and thus bind one's self to the ego, it is necessary to transcend them. While the seeker should initially cultivate sattva, his/her ultimate goal is to transcend the misidentification of the self with the gunas and to be unattached to both the good and the bad, the positive and negative qualities of all life.

When one rises above the three gunas that originate in the body; one is freed from birth, old age, disease, and death; and attains enlightenment. (BG 14:20).

The Yogic Model of Higher Consciousness

By now, you may be eager to get started on the practices that will enable you to reap the fruits of Nada Yoga. Please do restrain yourself for a little longer. There is plenty of time to practice and sufficient practices to quench your thirst for powerful spiritual techniques. Before starting a journey, it is best to understand the roadmap, learn to recognize certain landmarks, avoid the dangers and be prepared for any detours and obstructions.

In a similar manner, the potential practitioner should have a basic understanding of the spiritual models underlying a specific spiritual system of Self-Realization.

For the system of Nada Yoga, it is necessary to examine the following models before getting started. It is highly recommended that the practitioner return to study them over the course of time in order to gauge one's progress and to seek help for any wrong turns.

There are four models which have a direct and relevant bearing on all spiritual practice:

1. The progressive and iterative eightfold path of spiritual awakening annunciated by the yogic sage Patanjali.

2. The model of higher consciousness described by Patanjali in his Yoga Sutras.

3. The material involution model from gross to subtle matter and to subtlest matter that describes the evolution of the spiritual dimension. This Tattva model is necessary to understand the impact and effect of the techniques.

4. A subtle anatomy model covering the 5 bodies and the chakra/nadi system for understanding the operation of the techniques.

5. The program of subtle body purification given in the first three parts of the Hatha (Yoga) Pradipika is necessary to actualize the practice of Nada Yoga.

To understand the eight-fold path of Patanjali, it is necessary to remove the misconception that it is a ladder-like structure with each step leading to the next and one must move from one to the next in upward movement. Certainly, there is a measure of this step-wise progression in the model but the overall scheme is more like the spokes of a wheel and there is a cyclic nature the 'steps'. As the wheel rolls along, the steps are repeated.

After the yoga practitioner or sadhak has completed the cycle from step one to step eight, he or she will return to step one and so on. After each revolution, the steps become progressively deeper and higher in nature. After a number of revolutions, the speed reached blurs the steps and it becomes a continuous movement into higher consciousness.

Ultimately, step one and eight are merged and there is no longer any distinction between them – they contain each other. Another way to look at the model is from the objective to the subjective or from external to internal progressively. As we practice, we transcend the objective world and attain to pure subjectivity. Then we move back to the objective but in an enhanced mode. The goal is to achieve a merging of the objective-subjective and the external-internal polarities in unity that is yoga.

The first and most objective spoke of the wheel is Yama. This is popularly called the five restraints. They are:
- Satya: being truthful and refrain from lying
- Ahimsa: the refraining from harming other beings
- Asteya: refrain from stealing
- Brahmacharya: refrain from wasting one's energy on satisfying one's desires
- Aparigraha: refrain from being attached to the objective or subjective worlds

It is not my intention to go into depth about these five **Yama,** but to introduce them so that the practitioner has a basic concept. For more details, refer to my book – The Yoga of Purification and Transformation.

For our purposes here, we merely need to understand that:
1. these restrains apply to our everyday life. They need to be considered mentally, emotionally as well as physically, that is, we should refrain from harming others by thought, word or deed.
2. We are conditioned by our karmic burden in this

life to break these restraints.

3. If we can follow these restraints, we are making progress in overcoming our Karma.

4. These restraints are only limiting factors from our ego-centric point-of-view. As we progress spiritually, they become natural and second-nature as we become more and more attuned to our True Self.

5. These restraints are the basic attributes of our True Self and from that perspective, require no effort and are no longer restraints.

The second spoke in the wheel is that of **Niyama**. These are five positive attributes that we should develop. They are:

1. Saucha: purity in our emotional, mental and intentional continuum.

2. Santosha: contentment as an emotional and mental state.

3. tapas: control the five senses.

4. svadyaya: understanding and control of the mind.

5. Ishvar Pranidhana: integrating one's will to the universal will.

These attributes are more refined and less observable than the five Yama. They are transforming the emotional and mental attitudes of the spiritual practitioner. In the beginning, they require great effort to maintain even for a short time. However, as the student progresses in the other parts of the eight-fold path, these attributes become inherent in their psyche.
These attributes are the essence of the existential state of Being. A Self-Realized yogi, one who has attained to the unity consciousness with the true Self will have perfected these five

Niyama and the five Yama.

The Hatha (Yoga) Pradipika, upon which we will be relying on for the practices of Nada Yoga skips the Yama and Niyama and starts with Asana. This is because the yogis in the Middle Ages recognized that the ethical restraints and positive attributes had become obstacles for their students to begin their practice. The times were too turbulent and there were too many brutal invasions of the land and massacre of peoples to maintain the equinimity of ancient times.

Asana (Physical Postures)

Asana is the practice of physical postures. It is the most commonly known aspect of yoga for those unfamiliar with the other seven spokes of Patanjali's Yoga Sutra. The practice of moving the body into postures has the obvious benefits for improved health, strength, balance and flexibility. On a deeper level the practice of asana, which means "a steady or abiding posture" in Sanskrit, is used as a tool to calm the mind and move into the inner essence of being.

The challenge of maintaining a pose offers the practitioner the opportunity to explore and control all aspects of their emotions, and concentration bringing about a unity between the physical body and mind. Asana is a way of exploring our mental attitudes and strengthening our will as we learn to release and move into the state of grace that comes from creating balance between our material world and spiritual experience.

As one practices asana it helps to quiet the mind, becoming both a preparation for concentration as well as a means of concentration in itself. The physical nature of the yoga postures becomes a vehicle to expand the consciousness that pervades every aspect of our body.

The key to engendering this expansion of awareness and consciousness begins with the control of breath, the fourth limb called Pranayama. Patanjali tells us that the asana and the pranayama practices will bring about the desired state of health. The control of breath and bodily posture will harmonize the flow of energy in the organism, creating a fertile field for the evolution of the spirit.

Pranayama (Breath Expansion & Control)

Pranayama is the expansion, control, and directing of the breath. Pranayama controls the life-force energy (prana) within the body, in order to restore and maintain health and to promote evolution. When the in-flowing breath is neutralized or joined with the out-flowing breath, then perfect relaxation and balance of body activities are realized. In yoga, we are concerned with balancing the flows of vital forces, then directing them inward to the chakra system and upward to the crown chakra.

Pranayama, or breathing technique, is very important in yoga. It goes hand in hand with the asana or pose.

In the Yoga Sutra, the practices of pranayama and asana are considered to be the highest form of purification and self-discipline for the mind and the body, respectively. The practices produce the actual physical sensation of heat, called tapas, or the inner fire of purification. It is taught that this heat is part of the process of purifying the nadis, or subtle nerve channels of the body. This allows a more healthful state to be experienced and allows the mind to become calmer. As the yogi follows the proper rhythmic patterns of slow deep breathing "the patterns strengthen the respiratory system, soothe the nervous system and reduce carnal craving. As desires and cravings diminish, the mind is set free and becomes a fit vehicle for concentration.

Pratyahara (Sense Withdrawal)

Pratyahara means drawing back or retreat. The word ahara means "nourishment"; pratyahara translates as "to withdraw oneself from that which nourishes the senses." In yoga, the term pratyahara implies withdrawal of the senses from attachment to external objects. It can then be seen as the practice of non-attachment to sensory distractions as we constantly turn to the path of self-realization and achievement of internal peace.

In pratyahara we sever this link between mind and senses, and the senses are no longer tied to external sources. When the vital forces are flowing back to the center within, one can concentrate without being distracted by externals or the temptation to cognize externals. It means our senses stop living off the things that stimulate and no longer depend on these stimulants and are no longer fed by them.

Pratyahara needs to occur when we concentrate because we should be absorbed in the object of concentration. As long as the mind is so focused internally, the senses follow it.

Under normal circumstances the senses become our masters rather than being our servants. The senses entice us to develop cravings for all sorts of things. In pratyahara the opposite occurs: when we have to eat we eat, but not because we have a craving for food. In pratyahara we try to put the senses in their proper place, but not cut them out of our actions entirely. The senses become extraordinarily sharp when controlled.

What causes emotional imbalance? Each of us is responsible for creating our emotional imbalance since we are continuously influenced by outside events and sensations. We can never achieve the inner peace and tranquility. This is because he or she will waste much mental and physical energy in trying to suppress unwanted sensations and to heighten pleasurable sensations. Such efforts tied to the avoidance or attraction to sensations can lead to emotional imbalances and psychosomatic illnesses.

Patanjali says that the above process is at the root of human unhappiness and uneasiness. When people seek out yoga to find that inner peace which is so difficult to capture, they find that it was theirs all along. In this sense, yoga is nothing more than a process which enables us to stop and look at the processes of our own minds in order to understand the nature of happiness and unhappiness, and then be able to transcend them both.

Dharana (Concentration)

Dharana means "immovable concentration of the mind". The essential idea is to hold the concentration or focus of attention on one object. "When the body has been tempered by asanas, when the mind has been refined by the fire of pranayama and when the senses have been brought under control by pratyahara, the sadhaka (seeker) reaches the sixth stage, dharana. Here he is concentrated wholly on a single point or on a task in which he is completely engrossed." The mind has to be stilled in order to achieve this state of complete absorption In dharana we create the conditions for the mind to focus its attention on a single object or subject instead of going out in many different directions. Deep contemplation and reflection can create the right conditions, and the focus on this one point that we have chosen becomes more intense. We encourage one particular activity of the mind and, the more intense it becomes, the more the other activities of the mind fall away. The objective in dharana is to steady the mind by focusing its attention upon some stable entity. The objective is to stop the mind from wandering. The mind meanders through memories, dreams, or reflective though. It is necessary to achieve the mental state where the mind and ego are restrained. When the mind has become purified by yoga practices, it becomes able to focus efficiently on one subject or point of experience.

Dhyana (Absorptive Meditation)

The seventh spoke is Dhyana - it is perfect absorption. It involves concentration upon an object or subject of focus with the intention of knowing the truth about it. The concept holds that when one is absorbed in an object the mind is transformed into the shape of the object. In this way, when one focuses on the divine, one becomes more reflective of that aspect of the divine – know and live that aspect.

During dhyana of the universal spirit, the consciousness is further unified by combining clear insights into distinctions between objects and between the subtle layers of perception. One learns to differentiate between the mind of the perceiver, the means of perception, and the objects perceived.
As we fine-tune our concentration and become more aware of the nature of reality we perceive that the world is unreal. "The only reality is the universal Self, or Divine, which is veiled by Maya (the illusory power). As the veils are lifted, the mind becomes clearer. Unhappiness and fear – even the fear of death – vanishes. This state of freedom, or Moksha, is the goal of Yoga. It can be reached by constant enquiry into the nature of things. Meditation becomes our tool to see things clearly and perceive reality beyond the illusions that cloud our mind.

Samadhi (Unity Consciousness of Bliss)

The final spoke in the eight-fold path of Yoga is the attainment of Samadhi. Samadhi means "to bring together, to merge." There are a variety of samadhi states. In some states of samadhi the body and senses are at rest, as if asleep, while awareness is heightened in super-consciousness. In higher states of samadhi, called sahaj samadhi, it is possible to be in super-consciousness and still maintain the body and senses in operation.

During samadhi, we realize what it is to be an identity without differences, and how a liberated soul can enjoy pure awareness of this pure identity. The limited mind drops back into that unconscious pool from which it first emerged.

Samadhi is Yoga. There is an ending to the separation that is created by the "I" and "mine" of our illusory perceptions of reality. The mind does not distinguish between self and non-self, or between the object contemplated and the process of contemplation. The mind and the intellect have stopped and there is only the experience of consciousness, truth and bliss, Sat-Chid-Ananda.

The achievement of samadhi is a difficult task. For this reason the Yoga Sutra suggests the practice of asanas and pranayama as preparation for dharana, because these influence mental activities and create space in the crowded schedule of the mind. Once dharana has occurred, dhyana and samadhi can follow.

These eight spokes of yoga indicate a logical pathway that

leads to the attainment of physical, ethical, emotional, and psycho-spiritual health. Yoga does not seek to change the individual; rather, it allows the natural state of total health and integration in each of us to become a reality.

Benefits of Nada for Meditation

1. During meditation, the mind wanders and the seeker must focus his attention on an objective phenomenon to stop it from losing concentration. The nada sound is an ideal "internal" object for the attention to hold on to.

2. It has been observed that concentrating on nada has a purifying and calming effect on the mind and emotions.

3. As the seeker becomes more and more attuned to the higher vibration of nada, she discovers that she is slowly rising to higher and more luminous levels of consciousness.

4. By relying on the nada vibration as the meditative support and becoming attuned to its intensity and brightness, the seeker will become immediately aware when his attention has wavered and he has forgotten his self by becoming lost in his ordinary consciousness.

The Practice Of Nada Yoga

Time for Practice

One can practice nada yoga whenever one is free. Traditionally, it has been advised that between midnight and two a.m., the period free from the disturbing influences of external sound, is the best time for practice. Absence of light in the surroundings is also helpful for the practice. The key is to turn the mind inwards.

Nowadays, in practical householder terms, the best time is usually early morning just before going to work or late evening, about two hours after dinner.

Precautions

Some precautions should be borne in mind because nada yogic sadhana can bring about a manifestation of any sound. Sometimes, if the practitioner has a disturbed mind, there may be a buzzing in the ears throughout the day. Sometimes he may hear the sound of a bell or various other sounds. If the manifestation of these different sounds disturb the peace of the aspirant and continues to agitate the mind, the nada sadhana can be put on hold. Most of the time, with correct practice of nada yoga, inner sounds are developed in stages and are not heard at any other time during the waking period, unless the practitioner focuses on them.

According to Yogic Masters, the advanced nada yogi is capable of hearing a voice in the waking state if he is at a very advanced stage. It appears as if someone is whispering into his ears. This is a kind of siddhi - a power to hear the vibration from the source.

Guidelines for Practice

1. Regular practice
It is important to establish the habit of daily practice at a fixed time because the mind is more easily controlled and slowed down when it is conditioned to expect the practice.

2. Set aside a space for practice – although it is best to have a room for your meditation, it is not necessary. However, a partitioned or screened off space within a room that only you will use can be very helpful. Your practice sets up a vibration that can help to induce a quiet mind – this can be disturbed by others accessing the space.

3. The most effective times for meditation are at dawn and dusk. Just before sunrise, the mind is clear and undisturbed by your daily activities. It is more easily rewired during these times. If it is not possible to practice early in the morning, choose a time when you are relatively undisturbed and mind can be calmed – choose a time that can become a regular routine.

4. The best directions to face are east to align with the movement of the earth or north to align with the magnetic field.

5. For the actual Nada Meditation, sit in a comfortable and steady posture with head and neck erect but relaxed. This helps to steady the mind and promote concentration. Such a posture enables the energy currents to travel unimpeded from the base of the spine to the top of the head. The legs should form a triangle, a firm base for long duration – any cross-legged posture will work. If it is not possible to sit on the floor, then sitting on the edge of a chair or even lying down on your back are acceptable alternatives.

6. Calm the mind and practice slow deep breathing for a few minutes before commencing the meditation.

Sequence for Nada Sadhana

1. Asansas for purifying the body vessel
2. Mudras for controlling prana
3. Pranayamas for purifying the nadis and chakras as well as increasing the flow of prana
4. Pranaymas for awakening the kundalini
5. Jyoti or Shanmukhi Mudra for awakening to vibration, sound and light
6. Nada Meditation

Posture 1: Forward Bend

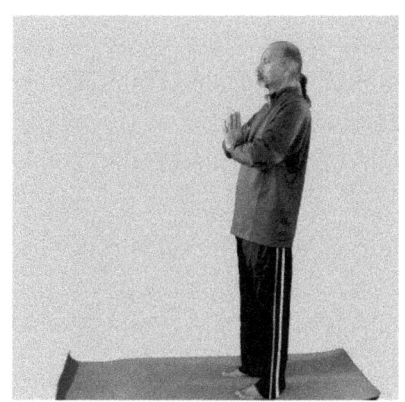

Stand with feet shoulder width apart. Clasp hands together at heart level. Centering oneself.

Kneel down gently. Take a few slow and deep breaths.

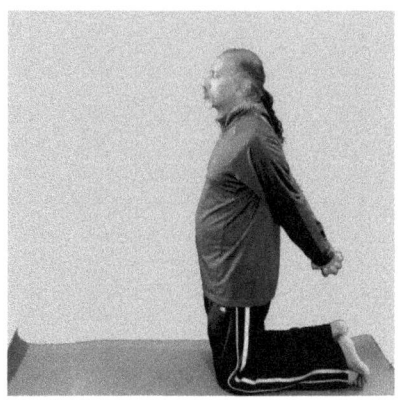

Clasp hands behind and bring shoulders together.

Sit down on your heals. Inhale to a count of 6 as you mentally chant the mantra "SAA"

Exhale to a count of 6 as you bend forward to touch the head to the floor. Mentally chant "Hum" during exhale.

As your head touches the floor or as you reach you position limit, hold the breath out for the count of 6.

Inhale as you raise your head up, still keeping your hands clasped. Mentally chant "SAA" for the count of 6.

Lean your head back as you hold your breath in for a count of 6. This finishes one round. Perform at least 3 rounds of the posture.

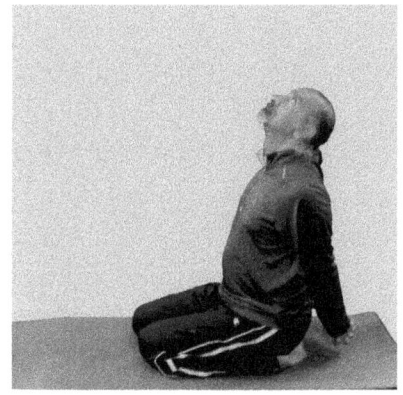

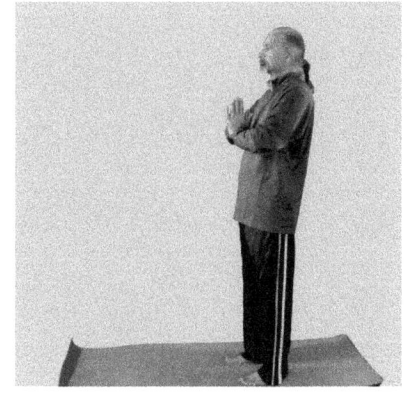

Return to standing position after completion of the posture.

Posture 2: Spinal Twist

Stand in the starting position with feet shoulder width apart and hands clasped at heart level.

Sit down with the legs crossed and take a few centering breaths.

Keeping the left leg on the floor, place your right foot over the left knee.

Place the left elbow over the right knee.

Clasp your right ankle with your left hand. Inhale to a count of 6 while mentally chanting "SAA"

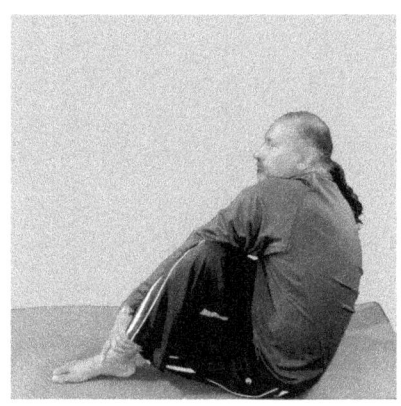

While holding your breath, twist your waist to the right and look towards your back. Hold for a count of 12.

Exhale to a count of 6 as you slowly release the twist and face forwards again. Mentally chant "HUM".

Release your hands from the ankle and the elbow from the knee.

Bend the right knee, keeping the leg on the floor. Place the left foot over the right knee and the right elbow over the left knee.

Clasp the left ankle with the right hand. Inhale for a count of 6 while mentallly chanting "SAA"

While holding the breath, turn your waist towards the left and face your back. Hold for a count of 12.

Exhale for a count of 6 as you release the twist and face the front. Chant "HUM" mentally as you exahle. This completes one round. Perform at least 3 rounds.

Posture 3: Cow-faced Pose

Assume the standing pose and then kneel down on the left knee.

Sit down towards the inside of the left leg.

Place right leg over the left thigh. Take a few centering breaths.

Raise your right hand as your inhale to a count of 6 while chanting "SAA".

Hold your breath as you bend your left hand behind your back.

Bend your right elbow so that the right hand can grasp the left hand. Hold for a count of 12.

The right hand and left hand are grasped at the back. A towel or band can be used if the hands cannot reach.

Release the hands and get up with right knee on the floor.

Sit down on the inside of the right leg and cross the left knee over the right. Take a few centering breaths.

Raise the left hand up as you inhale to a count of 6 while mentally chanting "SAA". Bend the right hand behind your back.

Hold your breath for a count of 12 while clasping the two hands together.

Clasping hands and holding breath. This is one round. Complete at least 3 rounds.

Posture 4: Camel Pose

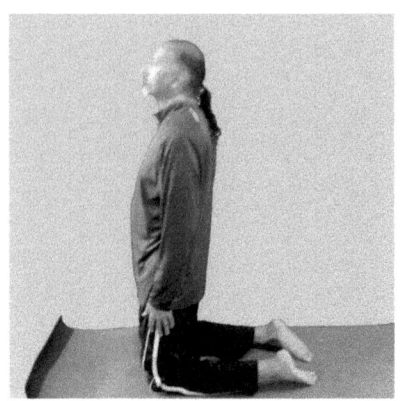

Assume the standing pose and lower yourself down on both knees.

Lean back and reach back with your hands and hold on to the corresponding ankles.

Lean further back as you perform rapid abdominal breathing for at least 30 seconds. Repeat "SAA" with every inhale and "HUM" with every exhale.

As your finish the last breath, you hold your breath out and raise your body up towards the front.

Continue the movement with hands in fist form and by the side. Head close the floor.

With the body curled up and breath held out, tighten all the muscles. Hold for a count of 12 and then relax.
Repeat sequence at least 3 times.

Breathing Exercise: Sun-Moon Breath

A. Preparation phase

1. *Cleansing the air-passages and lungs*:
   Sit comfortably in one of the recommended postures. Place your hands on your knees. Inhale a Complete Breath. Then pucker your lips and exhale vigorously through them in a series of short, sharp exhalations as you slowly lower your trunk and forehead as close to the floor as possible. Then slowly raise your head and trunk back up while slowly breathing in through the nostrils. Perform this three times.

2. *Alternate nadi-cleansing*:
   This is especially beneficial for those suffering from sinus congestion.

   Sit in a comfortable posture with your spine straight and your body relaxed.

   Slowly inhale through both nostrils, then pucker your lips and exhale all the air from your lungs with a series of dynamic exhalations, like a bellows action.

   Closing the right nostril with your right thumb, inhale gently through the left nostril. Then close your left nostril with the third finger of your right hand and exhale through your right nostril, with a series of short, sharp exhalation.

Continue with inhaling through the right nostril, and exhaling with force through the left. This completes one round. Start the cycle again with inhaling through both nostrils. Practice three rounds.

B. Purification Phase

3. *Basic Sun-Moon Purification*:
   This is the most important Prana Energy Training technique for purifying the energy channels and strengthening the nerves of the physical body. It purifies the blood and the brain cells, and also maintains equilibrium in the catabolic and anabolic processes in the body.

   By making the breath flow in each nostril in a balanced way, the pranic flow in the Sun and Moon channels become balanced. Under these balanced conditions, prana will flow into the central channel and the left and right brains are equally stimulated.

   Sit comfortably in one of the four recommended postures, with the head, neck and spine in a straight line. Keep a smile on your face and the body relaxed.

   Place your left hand on your left knee, relaxed, and form the right hand in nasik mudra. This is formed by folding the first two fingers towards the palm keeping the thumb and the last two fingers extended. Refer to figures 8 and 9.

First, exhale through both nostrils, and then close your right nostril with your thumb and inhale slowly and deeply through your left nostril. At the end of the inhalation, close your left nostril with your ring and little fingers, release your thumb from the right nostril and exhale through your right nostril. Next, inhale through your right nostril, then close it with your thumb and exhale through your left nostril.

Figure 8:
Sun-Moon Breath - closing right nostril

This completes one round. Practice only 6 rounds to begin with, then gradually increase to 12 rounds after a few weeks.

Figure 9:
Sun-Moon Breath: exhaling through the right nostril

4. *Advanced Sun-Moon Purification*:
   Add this part to your Prana Energy Training only after you have practiced the Basic technique for at least one month. This uses the same alternating breathing pattern

as in the Basic Sun-Moon Breath, adding the counting of the length of inhalation and exhalation, which was learned in Calming Breath [Part 1].

In the Calming Breath, we learnt to inhale and exhale to the same count. The relative ratios of breath inhalation, retention) and exhalation) are: 1:0:1:0 This means that there is no breath retention and that the exhalation is the same as that of the inhalation. For the Advanced Sun-Moon Breath, we use a ratio of 1:0:2:0, that is, the exhalation is twice as long as the inhalation. There is no holding of breath between inhalation and exhalation.

Begin with a minimum inhalation count of six and therefore an exhalation of twelve for the first week. Do not increase the count until you can practice this with comfort and ease, and then increase the count to 8 for inhale and 16 for exhale.

First, practice three rounds of inhaling and exhaling through the left nostril with the required ratio. Then perform three rounds of inhaling and exhaling through the right nostril with the same ratio. This helps to setup the rhythym of the breath.

Continue with the alternating or Sun-Moon breath. Apply nasik mudra, and inhale through the left nostril, counting the length of the inhalation. Exhale through the right nostril, making the exhalation twice as long as the inhalation. Breathe in through the right nostril, counting the length of the inhalation, and then exhale through the left nostril, making the exhalation twice as long as the inhalation. This is one round. Continue for a total of six rounds.

Caution on the holding of breath

There is a lot of misunderstanding about the practice of breath retention or holding of breath during Prana Energy Training. This is due to the popularization of advanced *Yogic* texts, which appear to promote this practice indiscriminately. In general, holding of breath can put a stress on your heart and circulatory system, elevating the blood pressure several times above normal, which can result in ruptured blood vessels or a stroke.

What may not be clear from books is that beginners in *Yoga* are not taught the holding of breath, until they have had years of practice in strengthening the body, circulatory system and nervous systems, and only after authorization and personal supervision from their teachers. When holding of breath is taught, it should always be accompanied by the practice of the muscular locks or bandhas. The holding of breath is not necessary or even recommended for the therapeutic purpose of Prana Energy Training. It is an important aspect of the mystical side of breath practice for attaining higher states of consciousness.

It is my personal experience and observation, that most breathing techniques do not require the active and forced breath retention, but will over time, increase the natural pause between the inhaled breath and the exhaled breath. This natural pause does not put a strain on the heart.

Sun Moon Breath

In realms of subtle energy, find grace,
Where prana flows in channels, left or right,
In pingala, solar energy life embrace,
Thru ida, lunar's soothing, mental light.

In alternate breath, balance we seek.
Nadi Shodana, the practice profound.
Sun and Moon, harmonize at peak,
With concentrated will all energies resound.

When in balance, kundalini awakes,
Rising through sushumna, the central path.
Its ascent, the sacred serpent makes,
Nada, the divine sound of mystical heart.

In realms of mind and energy's might,
Sounds the mystic serpent taking flight.

Brahmari Nada Pranayama

1. Sit in any comfortable meditation asana or posture – the recommended posture is siddhasana. The back and head should be straight with hands on the knees in chin mudra. Close your eyes and relax the body, focusing on the mid-eyebrow for a minute or so.

2. Raise your arms sideways with bent elbows. Insert your index fingers into the ears to plug them. Try to be comfortable. You can also try to use your thumbs to close the ear flaps instead – experiment to see which works best for you.

3. Slowly move your awareness down to the base of the spine. Inhale the breath upward inside the spinal passage in the subtle sushumna nadi (central channel), from the muladhara (root chakra) to the ajna or third-eye center. Hold the breath at the third-eye center for about five seconds and then slowly exhale down the spine back to the root center. During the exhalation, you are making a long continuous humming sound (mm-mm-mm) like that of a bee. This humming sound should continue for the whole duration of the exhalation. When the breath reaches the root chakra, you start a new inhalation up the spine. One inhalation and one exhalation completes one round and you should practice at least twelve rounds and not more than eighteen.

4. During the inhalation, focus your attention on the energy movement in the spinal channel. Throughout the exhalation, try to experience the vibration in the body caused by the humming sound.

5. After finishing the twelve to eighteen rounds, keep your eyes and ears closed. Bring your attention to any internal sounds. Concentrate on the internal sounds to the exclusion of all else – the sound will become louder and more distinct over time. As your sensitivity increases, you will become aware of a second fainter sound behind the one you've been concentrating on. Transfer your attention to this fainter and more subtle sound. When this second sound becomes louder over time, you will again become aware of a third fainter sound beyond it. At that time, follow that fainter sound. This process of discovering more and more subtle sounds may continue for some time.

6. Open your ears to end the practice. Let go of the awareness of the internal sounds and sit quietly for a few minutes. Be one with yourself. Become aware of your breath and then your body posture and finally the sounds around you. Then you can open your eyes and slowly get up.

Figure 10: Brahmari Nada Pranayama

Shanmukhi Mudra

This is essentially a technique to master the art of pratyahara, which means withdrawal of mind and prana (life-force energy) from the objects perceived through the five senses.

This technique has various names to emphasize its different aspects -Jyoti mudra, where Jyoti means "inner starlight" and mudra means "seal". It is also called Yoni Mudra - Yoni means "womb" or "source." A third name is Shanmukhi mudra, because shan means "seven" and mukhi means "orifice" or "mouth," and in this technique, the seven orifices are sealed so that the inner star of the Soul can be perceived, passing through which the Conscious Seer experiences Cosmic Consciousness.

According the Mahayogi Gorakhnath:

> As a Tortoise Withdraws it's Limbs
> into it's shell so also let the yogi
> introvert his senses by jyoti mudra
> and penetrate the Inner Stargate

By this mudra your mind is brought to a state of relaxed absorption whereby pratyahara (sense withdrawal) ensues and makes the it easier to tune in to the unstruck sound or nada. This state of sense withdrawal occurs because of the pressure of the fingers upon specific nerves and acupressure points.

There are also physical benefits of yoni mudra because it stimulates the vagus nerves through pressure on the ear canals with the thumbs. The stimulation of these nerves brings about a dominance of the parasympathetic nervous system thereby lowering ones metabolic threshold, giving rise to deeper meditation experiences. It is important to refrain from imagining the light and sound.

The three locks or Tribandha

Contract the muscles in the region between the anus and genitals and lift them up vertically towards the navel. The practice of contracting the anal sphincter muscle is the first step in the practice of the Mulabandha or root lock

When holding the breath, pull the whole abdominal region back towards the spine and lift it upwards. Squeeze the abdominal organs towards the spine. This abdominal loc

In the third lock, slowly bend the head forwards towards the chest. Do not strain the neck. Keep the muscles of the throat and neck soft. Keeping the head centred and bring it down so that the chin rests evenly in between the collarbones. Do not force the chin on the chest; lift the chest to meet the descending chin. Keep the centre of the head and chin in alignment with the middle of the sternum.

These three locks help to focus the prana to the third eye centre and keeps it from dispersing during the holding of breath.

Practice

Sitting in a comfortable position with the back straight. Raise your hands and close your eyes with your index fingers, with 1/4th of the index finger on the eyelashes and 3/4th on the curvature of the eye socket.
Then with your thumbs, close your ears, putting the pressure of the thumbs directly above the ear lids, where the skull and jawbone join. This ensures a complete closure of sound.

The third phase would be to further shut your closed mouth with your ring and pinky fingers.

Take a slow and deep breath. Then, block either side of your nostrils with both your middle fingers. The seven orifices of your senses being shut, hold your breath as long as you comfortably can (about 30 seconds)

While holding your breath, apply the three locks or bandhas. Focus on the third eye and merge any sounds with the light. Hold as long as comfortable and then remover your fingers from your nostrils, slowly exhaling.

This is the completion of one Yoni or Jyoti mudra. You must practice a minimum of three such rounds.

Figure 11a: Hand Position for Shanmukhi

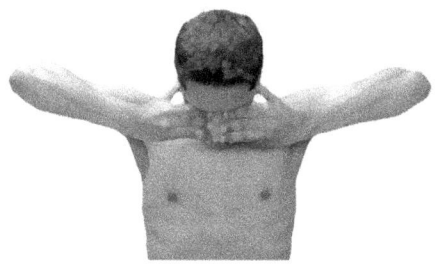

Figure 11b: Applying the Locks in Shanmukhi

Practice for the Manifestation of Nada

Sit down on a firm cushion in a squatting position, placing the soles of the feet on the ground with the elbows resting on the knees or thighs. For some a lower cushion will be comfortable and for others a higher one. The most important point here is that the coccyx and the perineum should be pressed against the cushion at the point of muladhara, and therefore it should be round and hard. If this is very uncomfortable for you, then adopt any steady posture including sitting on a chair.

Chant Om aloud for a few minutes followed by a minute in a whispering manner and finally mentally.

Plug both the ears with the index fingers. Bring your consciousness to the back of the head (bindu) and try to listen or be aware of any sound that is internal. This internal sound may resemble anything. It may be like an electric current or a gurgling sound, the ocean waves or a bell ringing. It may also be the sound of a flute, the rhythm of a guitar or the sound of birds chirping in the evening at the time of sunset. It might be in the form of an awareness of the distant ocean or the sound of a thunderbolt. Or it might even be the vision of a starry night devoid of any sound. These internal sounds are to be discovered by the practitioner.

If it is difficult to discover a sound at bindu, focus your awareness at the crown chakra (sahasrara) or the third-eye center. Discover the sound instead of imagining it. Withdraw the senses and make your mind one-pointed, then discover the first sound and pursue it up to the end. One inner sound of nada should be followed to the extent where it becomes clearer and as soon as it is clear and prominent, another sound (a different sound altogether) may be heard and felt in the background.

When you discover the second sound, give up the first one and follow the second, which is usually subtler. For instance, close your ears and listen to the first sound- it may be thunder or a drumming. Keep on listening to it. When it becomes completely clear and distinct, another sound may manifest behind, such as the sound of an electric current. Now, allow your consciousness to follow this sound. When it is completely distinct, clear and dominates, the first sound will have disappeared.

Don't get attached to any particular sound. Let your awareness flow. It will naturally flow upwards to higher and higher realms.

This process continues with subtler and subtler vibrations. There is no need to keep count of the sounds. Keep flowinguntil the mind is completely still and the consciousness is completely devoid of the contents of the mind - it is pure awareness.

Allow your awareness to penetrate even deeper still. Be aware of absolute stillness. Experience the whole of creation inside which is beyond intellectual perception. Feel that your whole being is filled with divine vibrations - cosmic sound. Listen to the music of the transcendental spheres. This music is without beginning and without end. It has no cause. It is the unstruck sound which is also known as the anahad nada.

Beconme one with the nada - there is no subject/object differentioan and be at peace and bliss.

When you are ready to end the practice. Bring your awareness back to the physical dimension. Become aware of the slow and steady flow of the breath. Become aware of the sensation of the physical body. Be aware of heat or coolness, comfort, or discomfort, and all the other experiences of the body. Slowly begin to externalize your mind. Listen to the sounds in the external environment. Become aware of your surroundings. Now breathe in deeply and chant Om three times. Slowly begin to move the body and open the eyes.

Advanced Topics

Higher Consciousness - Samadhi

In his Yoga Sutras Patanjali describes three processes that will lead us to the supreme state of consciousness – dharana, dhyana and samadhi.

- Dharana means concentration. In concentration we direct our consciousness towards a single object (for example, a Bija Mantra), withdrawing it completely from all other things. For this it is crucial that we focus our attention totally on a single point.
- Dhyana is meditation. This is the next step after concentration when the "I" begins to dissolve in the object. This is the preliminary stage to samadhi. One cannot "learn" meditation. When body and mind are correctly attuned and have become quiet and pure the meditative state occurs by itself – just as sleep overcomes us by itself when we go to bed in the evening.
- Samadhi is the unity consciousness in which knower, knowledge and object of knowledge unite. I would like to know. I am the knower. I would like the knowledge. With the union of these three points of view the certainty and experience of "I am that – SO HAM" occurs.

Unity Consciousness cannot be experienced by the intellect alone - only when knowledge, knower and object become one. In the realization of the unity of SO HAM (I am that) all questions are answered and all desires fulfilled - the knower no longer exists, knowledge is no longer desired and there is no knowledge to acquire or any object to know. In the fullness of perfect existence all desires are extinguished.

To have this experience means realization of the truth – Self-Realization and God-Realization. Shankaracharya praised the God-Realized, liberated consciousness in the following stotra:

> I am not this mind, nor intellect, ego or consciousness,
> Nor the Gyana Indriyas or the Tattvas.
> My form is pure consciousness and absolute bliss
> I am chidananda rupa, Shiva, the Supreme Self.
> I am neither the five Pranas nor the seven Dhatus,
> Nor the five Koshas, nor this bundle of Karmas
> I am chidananda rupa, Shiva, the Supreme Self.
> In me exists neither attachment nor duality,
> Neither greed nor jealousy, neither hate nor anger.
> I have nothing to do with the illusion of the ego,
> And also I am not bound by the four laws of the Purushartha
> I am chidananda rupa, Shiva, the Supreme Self.
> I have neither sin nor virtue, nothing to do with
> either happiness or sorrow,
> Or with Mantras, pilgrimages, the Vedas or ceremonies
> I am neither the food, nor the one nourished,
> nor the enjoyer
> I am chidananda rupa, Shiva, the Supreme Self.
> I am the atma, immortal and unborn
> Time, space and death have no power over me
> I have neither father nor mother,
> neither relatives nor friends
> No Guru and no student
> I am chidananda rupa, Shiva, the Supreme Self.

> I am desire-less and formless.
> I exist in all living beings
> I am not bound, nor require liberation
> My form is truth, consciousness and bliss
> I am chidananda rupa, Shiva, the Supreme Self.

What is the nature of the consciousness of one whose Self is established in reality and truth? How do they see others? How do they see their surroundings? What thoughts and emotions exist in the consciousness of such a realized one? How do they live in the world?

Realized souls can only be recognized with the eyes of the soul. Outwardly they appear exactly the same as anyone else. They eat, sleep, speak, laugh and go about their daily duties the same as others. But with deeper reflection the differences are noticeable. A peaceful nature, all-understanding goodness, purity, splendor and a quiet dignity radiate from a God-Realized soul.

The unity consciousness of Samadhi and the liberation of Self-Realization occur in the thousand-petalled lotus (Sahasrara or crown chakra). It opens when we follow one of the Yoga paths with perseverance and devotion – the path of Raja Yoga or Kriya Yoga with discipline and practice, the path of Karma Yoga with selfless service, the path of Bhakti Yoga with devotion to God, or the path of Gyana Yoga with study and renunciation. It is also said that we need Guru Kripa or the grace of the divine teacher.

The Masters have always counseled that: "One should not

change one's inner vision". This means that we should remain faithful to the chosen path, Master or Ishta-devata (aspect of divinity) and not constantly change our beliefs or objectives. To reach the top of a mountain we should stay focused on the goal and move forward – do not to turn back or go around in circles.

Beware of the ego – never think that you are so great that you do not need guidance or discipline. It is a trap that some fall in – to think of oneself as the divine spirit, when one has not yet realized that truth – it is pure theory and does not align with reality.

Many things in life nourish the ego and cause a person to feel pride - youth, beauty, money, education, ethnic origin and social status. These are superficial factors caused by our previous good karma. We should make good use of these positive factors to help ourselves and others so that we can decrease our future bad karma. Instead, the ego influences us to abuse our good karma and produce bad karma for our future.

It is good to remember we have no control over even our own body - today strong and healthy, tomorrow perhaps weak and ill. It is best to surrender yourself to the Divine and devote ourselves to righteousness. We must clear our karmas and purify the ego so that he self or jiva can detach itself from the five koshas that veil it and hamper its free development. In this phase of development we are occasionally in an extremely vulnerable and disagreeable state – comparable to a snake when it sheds its skin. During the period that the snake is shedding its skin it can see nothing, is almost unable to move and also cannot eat. However, once it is fully released from the old sheath it is free and in full possession of its power. And so, when the jiva soul has rid itself of all fetters and reaches the Sahasrara Chakra, in that same moment it perceives the full light of truth.

It is difficult to determine what came first – the seed or the tree, the fruits or the karma. For eternity, the seed has grown from the plant, and the plant from the seed, in an inexhaustible sequence. In the same way an action produces a karmic reaction, and this reaction again causes an action. Karmas and samskaras (karmic traces) have, from the beginning, been inextricably linked to one another. But through Yoga we can free ourselves from this cycle. The fire of Yoga burns up karmas.

Only when all the "seeds" of the Karmas and Vasanas (desires, wishes) have been roasted and burnt in the "fire of Yoga" can they no longer sprout. Only then does the door to liberation open to the aspirant. Because from then on one's actions produce no new samskaras in one's consciousness, and therefore no more effects for subsequent lives. With the dissolution of the ego – when the distinction of "I" and "you" no longer exist – the sanchit karma ((karma from earlier lives) also dissolves. But the prarabdha karma (karma that has become "ripe" in this life and has already begun to work) is different. This continues to discharge itself.

The following simile can serve as an example: When a turning wheel suddenly comes off, it continues to turn freely for a while before it finally comes to a standstill - this is how it is with karma. The root of birth and death – ignorance – is in fact destroyed, but the plant (the present life) still exists for some time.

Self-Realization is not a "final state" — it is a new beginning. It is the end of our ignorance. It is the end of our childhood and as we grow in consciousness we should take up greater responsibilities. Whoever has acquired knowledge and experience through study applies this in their profession for the benefit of others. So it is also when someone has attained Unity Consciousness and knowledge through Samadhi, he or she should give back to the rest of humanity.

Some Yogis withdraw from the activities of society and live as hermits far away from civilization. But they work spiritually for the benefit of the world through prayer and meditation. Their existence is itself a blessing for the world. Even the wind when it blows over the body of a jivanmukta is filled with Divine energy and radiation, and spreads harmony, happiness and peace everywhere it blows.

Other Realized Souls, though, go amongst people to teach them the truth. Even though they are liberated and unattached they give up the joy of heaven and return again to world in order to help living beings. To help others mentally and spiritually is a wonderful task — and at the same time a great art that requires deep understanding and comprehensive knowledge. For as long as we do not possess the insight and experience of a realized soul we should take care that we are not pulled back into Maya ourselves when we would like to help someone.
We are able to experience two types of Samadhi consciously -savikalpa samadhi and nirvikalpa samadhi.

Savikalpa means "with movement (of the mind)". This type of samadhi is also known as sabija samadhi (with seed) and savichara samadhi (with differentiation). In savikalpa samadhi emotions, thoughts and desires still exist – partly conscious and partly as subconscious or unconscious karmic seeds. But in nirvikalpa samadhi (nirbija or nirvichara samadhi) no more thoughts whatsoever exist - not one "seed" of a desire or karma remains.

If we imagine a lake that is mirror-smooth and motionless, when a pebble is thrown into the water, circular ripples are created that reproduce and spread outwards. This represents every situation, every impression in our lives – 'waves' are produced in our minds, just as with the pebble thrown into the water, and these reproduce and spread in our consciousness. We cannot estimate just how much gravel and debris is submerged in our consciousness - that is why it can take such a long time for all disruptive factors (kleshas and vikshepas) to be raised, purified and cleared from the depths of our subconsciousness. Once this happens and the mind again becomes still, we are able to advance to the Unity Consciousness.

The expression 'savikalpa samadhi' is related to sankalpa and vikalpa (a wish or resolution made and then dismissed). Just as a child builds a sandcastle, then soon afterwards destroys it and begins to build again, so in our imagination we create an entire world that we identify with and also experience. Then in the next moment when we come up with something else we destroy it – and so it continues non-stop.

To watch a child playing in the sand is entertaining and amusing for a short while. And so it is for a sage, a wise person, who watches with interest and is frequently astonished by how people seem to constantly build 'sandcastles' in their lives, and when one collapses to patiently begin to build the next.

Just as waking passes imperceptibly into sleep and sleep into dream, so we arrive at our first experience of savikalpa samadhi – inner enlightenment.

Enlightenment already begins in the agya chakra and the bindu chakra. The closer we come to the sahasara chakra, the more radiant the light becomes, until ultimately all forms dissolve and our inner space is filled with a radiant light, brighter than a thousand suns. We perceive a wonderful, all-pervasive sound (like the sound of OM sung by a thousand voices), and the door to the Infinite opens before our inner eye.

We all wish for spiritual experiences. But when the door of the sahasrara chakra opens for us we are like the swan ready to take flight, uncertain as to whether it should fly out into freedom or remain in the well-known surroundings. This is exactly how we feel when the Brahmarandhra opens. Even though this is what we have longed for and aimed at, it requires courage to take the next step when we are standing on the threshold.

It now lies with us whether we would like to continue with this experience or again withdraw to normal consciousness. For a seeker whose heart is filled with a burning desire for the divine light the meditation is not disturbed and continues.

The next level of samadhi is reached in the heavenly realms. On this level we can meet divine incarnations, liberated and God-Realized Saints and Masters. In line with our faith and the image of the Divine that we carry within us, each of us has different visions and experiences at this level of samadhi. Though, generally, it means that we have reached a heavenly sphere where we are joyfully welcomed. Here we can have many beautiful experiences. We meet the divine masters and return again to the 'normal' world with wisdom and knowledge.

Savikalpa samadhi brings us wonderful 'heavenly' experiences. Afterwards we can almost become addicted to them. But, gradually it becomes clear to us that we are unable to attain liberation in this way as we are still moving in other levels of consciousness. Then we again begin to strive for Realization and are finally guided to nirvikalpa samadhi.

Nirvikalpa samadhi is the state of pure bliss and absolute peace. It is not possible to describe this state as it is beyond all descriptions. In this state, the jivatma quenches its lifelong thirst for fulfillment in unit with the Atma. It releases itself from the limitations of individuality and merges with the divine Self, the supreme Consciousness. It experiences itself as the "center" of the Universe – as Atma, the spirit.

There is no suffering, no pain and no problems in the Divine Consciousness – everything is perfect and complete (purna). There are no wishes, no longing – no knower, no object and no knowledge; neither time nor space. There is only undivided existence – pure Being. The identification with the individual person and individuality dissolves in the all-encompassing Self.

Many people maintain that someone who has attained nirvikalpa samadhi, and therefore moksha, cannot live much longer. However, it is said that there are two types of realization. Some experience God-Realization (Atma Gyana) with full consciousness and continue to live afterwards as a jivanmukta (realized and liberated soul) in order to pass their knowledge on. Others, however, experience enlightenment and liberation only when they leave the body. Qualitatively there is no difference. Those who attain Moksha at the end of their mortal life are liberated and realized in the same way as those who have attained God-Realization during their earthly existence.

Nirvikalpa Samadhi is a state of indescribable happiness, from which we no longer want to return, and from where we can see no reason whatsoever why we should come back. We are everywhere – there is no place where we need to go. Who should return? From where, and to where?

Nevertheless many decide to bring their consciousness back into the body. Out of pure compassion they voluntarily renounce remaining in the bliss of samadhi consciousness, and stay in the world to help innumerable souls who are still in the sorrowful condition of ignorance.

The liberated ones are forever free from the chains of karma, which also means they are no longer subject to the cycle of birth and death. All the same, a few of them continue to return to the earth of their own free will - their only goal is to help other beings to attain liberation - only one who is free can free others.

Obstacles to Higher Consciousness and Remedies

There are three afflictions that hinder the aspiring soul during its journey of spiritual development. These are mala, vikshepa and avarana.
- Mala means impurity, physical as well as mental
- Vikshepa are the internal and external disturbances that plague us
- Avarana is the curtain of "not knowing" that clouds our consciousness – it is our basic ignorance

There is an allegory to illustrate our condition: A coin lies on the bottom of a bowl filled with water. If the water is dirty (mala), also turbulent (vikshepa) and, on top of that, is covered by a cloth (avarana) we cannot see the coin at the bottom of the vessel. Steps taken in isolation do not help. If we only remove the cloth our vision will still be obstructed by the waves. And even if the waves subside we are still unable to discern the coin because the water is polluted and cloudy. Then what to do? All three obstacles must be removed. Firstly we must take the cloth away, then filter and purify the water, and lastly quieten the waves. Then the coin can be seen clearly and raised to the surface.

Mala are our impure thoughts. They obscure and darken our mind. We are mistaken if we think that no-one can read our thoughts. We know exactly what we are thinking. "Freedom of thought" is our birthright, but we should not forget that every thought, as well as every action, comes back to us as karma.

External dirt is simple to remove, but inner impurities stick in the depths of our consciousness and are not so easily disposed of. To purify our body we need very little time – less than an hour, but we may require several lifetimes to purify our consciousness.

Vikshepa are disturbances that can stem either from the outer world or our inner world. We can protect ourselves and take precautions against external disturbances like noise, heat or cold. This is not the case with attacks from inside - such as fears and anxiety complexes. These are only prevented with difficulty. Nervousness, worry and annoyance are internal disturbances that churn up our mind and obstruct us until we are able to get to their root cause.

Hidden within us lie six very special abilities that help us overcome the influences of these barriers of mala, vikshepa and avarana. What are these assets that we can cultivate? To discover them requires keen self-observation and training of the consciousness. First we must find out what prevents us from discovering these inner friends and helpers.

We are hampered by the four inner foes:
- Kama – passion
- Krodha – anger
- Moha – delusion
- Lobha – greed

Moha lays the foundation stone for kama, krodha and lobha. Delusion is the main cause of our mental, psychic or physical suffering and our attachments. It is the reason for depression, fear, jealousy and sadness. Attachment is always connected with fear. Even when we are happy in the present moment the fear of losing that which we believe is absolutely necessary for our happiness sits deeply within us. The attempt to safeguard and increase our possessions strengthens and nurtures passion and desire within us. The fear of loss leads subsequently to the eruption of anger, jealousy and hostility.

Naturally we should look after and care about our possessions. Certainly we should love and take care of our children, partner and friends. But, it is important to respect the freedom of everyone - to make nobody dependent upon us, and also not to become dependent upon anyone. Attachment is like a spider's web that holds us firmly and stifles us. It is not my intent to say that we are not allowed to own things or we should leave our family and friends. On the contrary! I wish everyone a prosperous and happy life - but we should not forget that after death we cannot take even one coin with us, and that all worldly relationships are temporary.

Through the practice of Yoga and following ethical principles we are able to purify the four antahkaranas (mind, consciousness, intellect and ego), to overcome false attachments and the other qualities mentioned above, and to transform their destructive energy into the good. We can then cultivate and develop the six treasures that can help us overcome the four inner foes and the three fundamental afflictions.

The six attributes that we need to cultivate as antidotes are:
- Shama
- Dama
- Sharaddha
- Titiksha
- Uparati
- Samadhana

Shama is inner silence and calmness. It is peace! We achieve this as we withdraw the mind and senses from the bustle of the external world and focus on the inner Self – this is enabled by the practice of pratyahara during our yogic practice. Dama means self-control. When we rein in the senses, thoughts and emotions with the higher mind (buddhi), so that they do not gallop away like wild horses, we are able to avoid ill-considered actions and spare ourselves from the ensuing problems and suffering.

Sharaddha is faith. It is a trust - something that is absolutely fundamental to spiritual as well as all worldly relationships. Where trust is missing, doubt grows and gradually destroys love. Doubt is like 'sand in a salad'. A salad that has grains of sand mixed in with it is inedible, even though it may still appear to be delicious. Therefore remove your doubts and begin to trust. However, be careful to vet the truth of falsehoods before you place your faith.

Who should you trust? We should have faith in ourselves first of all. Many people have lost their self-confidence. Through the rediscovery of your inner treasures you also regain your self-confidence.

Next, have faith in your path and your purpose so that nothing or no-one can undermine it or dissuade you in any way. The way to perfection requires unconditional trust. Once you have decided upon a path, do not allow yourself to be discouraged by difficulties. Be deeply committed to the attainment of what you have resolved to do, and say to yourself with inner certainty: 'I will make it.' Do not think 'I will try it' - with this type of thinking you cripple yourself. Courageously seize the opportunities that fate offers you and place the outcome of your efforts in the hands of the Divine.

Thirdly, have absolute faith in your Master (if you are blessed to have one) – whether he or she is an internal guide or manifested externally. If you constantly doubt, then you are unable to see the truth even if it is directly before your eyes. Shraddha is primal trust, such as that between a mother and her child. A baby stops crying as soon as the mother takes it in her arms because it feels safe and secure. Whoever possesses this natural capacity to trust is happy and successful in life. You are only able to recognize the truth when you show unconditional trust in the Master, just like a child to its mother.

Uparati means to rise above things by not being dependent or being afraid. When you face everything with a positive attitude you cannot really be harmed because you are able to draw valuable lessons from everything, even accidents. Fear and problems always arise when we are afraid of losing something. A wealthy person who is surrounded by guards, bolts and padlocks is, in reality, a prisoner of his possessions.

In the principles of Raja Yoga it is said: "You should not accumulate possessions." Rise above worldly things and practice renunciation – not as a painful turning away from the world, but as a liberating act of turning towards the Divine. Mahatma Gandhi also said: "Renounce and enjoy". This is an important rule of life.

Titiksha is equanimity and inner strength. Everyone is aware that they will continue to face obstacles and difficulties in life. When was our existence ever completely free of problems? Don't give in to your fears even if a situation appears to be hopeless. Remember that nothing lasts forever. Only the Self is unchanging and eternal. Everything else is changeable and transitory because time continues to march on inexorably. The body is changing every second - just as thoughts, feelings and situations also continue to change. Never give in to despair, even if bad things are happening to you. Pray for titiksha, inner strength, courage and steadfastness.

Samadhana means inner composure and is the ability to remain focused on one's goal. Never lose sight of the goal. If disturbances and resistance surface, sit yourself down quietly, close your eyes and carefully think about the situation. If you feel a surge of malice or rage building within you do not act at once. Remain detached and merely observe your emotions.

A great saint said: "When the waves are high one should not dive into the sea for pearls."

Therefore wait until the inner waves have subsided, and then carefully and calmly ask yourself:

- What have I done? – Why have I acted so?
- What have I thought? – Why have I thought so?
- What do I think now? – Why do I think so?
- What should I think? – How should I act?

Further inquire of yourself:

- How important was it?
- Why was it so important?

Or

- Was it at all important?
- What have I lost?
- Have I really lost anything?
- Was it of importance for my eternal happiness?
- You can never lose what is important for eternal happiness - therefore, in reality you have lost nothing.

The second aspect of samadhana is to reflect on the sense and reason for existence:
- Who has created this world and for what purpose?
- Where do I come from and where do I go to?
- What is reality and what is unreality?
- What is my purpose in life?

Therefore, on a general level, samadhana means to withdraw

and observe. When the inner waves have subsided we can dive deeply within ourselves. Only in this way are we able to recognize the truth, the reality, and understand the sense of all difficulties and suffering. When we are able to withdraw the mind from external things, we can connect with the higher consciousness within ourselves and know the answers to all our questions.

Nada in the Koshas

These sounds which are heard are true. They are the symbols of the content of the mind and of consciousness. The mind rests on these symbols and it goes in quickly with their help. These sounds are experiences of the deeper layers of consciousness belonging to annamaya kosha, pranamaya kosha and manomaya kosha. These sounds are not imaginary. They may be understood as the vibrations of different spheres of one's existence. The physical, pranic, mental, supra-mental and the ananda or atmic are the five spheres of one's existence. In different spheres of existence different sounds are heard. There are physical sounds first, but when consciousness becomes fine and transcends the physical plane, it will come in touch with the subtle sounds of the movements of pranic consciousness in the physical body.

The entire range of human consciousness is divided into three, or subdivided into five parts. The conscious state consists of the annamaya and the pranamaya koshas, and these two bodies are made up of food and of prana. The second sphere of the personality is comprised of manomaya and vigyanamaya koshas and mainly contains mental and astral matter. The third dimension of consciousness is the realm of anandamaya kosha, which is full of bliss.

In the practice of nada yoga, the manifestation of nada takes place in accordance with the relation established between the mind and the other spheres of consciousness. For instance, if the mind or consciousness is rooted in the physical body, by closing your ears you will hear the sounds or vibrations produced by the movements of the heart, lungs, brain, blood circulation and the process of metabolism and catabolism that are going on inside the body.

If consciousness has penetrated the pranamaya kosha, you will hear many more sounds. And if the mind has gone deeper into the anandamaya kosha, then all other sounds will disappear and in its place the effect of nada yoga will remain.

Anahad Nada and Anahata Nada

What is anahad nada? No one has been able to tell even till this day. Some say that is the cosmic sound of Om. Others say it is like brahmari, a sound resembling the unceasing and unbroken sound of the honeybee. Some say that it is the beat of the heart.

Some people call it anahad, while others call it anahat. These two words convey two different meanings. Anahat derives from 'an' + 'aahat'. 'An' means 'no', 'aahat' means 'that which is striking, hammering or beating'. Therefore, anahat means 'no beating or striking of two things'. Usually a sound is produced by two things striking against each other, but anahat is a sound which is not produced by striking. It is spontaneous and automatic. Some scholars say that the nada is anahad. 'An' means 'no' and 'hada' means 'boundary' or 'compound'. Hence, anahad means 'without any limit, without any boundary,' or 'without any specification'. It is a sound upon which no limits can be put. It can be any sound.

Nada Yoga and Gorakhnath

The great guru Gorakhnath, disciple of yogi Matsyendranath, gives a description of nada yoga. He writes, "Oh sadhu! Do japa of Soham. That japa should not be done through the mind. It should be done through the consciousness, so that even when you are engaged in your day-to-day activities, you should be aware of 21,6000 rhythms of your breath throughout the 24 hours of the day, at the rate of 15 or 19 rounds per minute (which means 900 and more breaths per hour). Anahad nada will emerge and will manifest on its own." He says further, "There will be light in the spinal cord. The solar system of the surya nadi will be awakened. You will feel an indescribable vibrating sound from every pore of your body and that will be like Om or Soham."

The Ultimate Nada

The ultimate nada that manifests in the highest sphere of consciousness is indescribable. It is a sound coming from the sphere beyond the anandamaya kosha. A nada yogi believes that the actual point where the individual consciousness fuses with the cosmic consciousness is in the highest state of nada. The aspirant or sadhaka realizes his higher consciousness in nada and sees the whole universe in the form of sound.

Nada and Turiya

Turiya is a state of consciousness often referred to as the fourth state of consciousness, beyond waking, dreaming, and deep sleep. It is a state of pure consciousness, beyond the limitations of the mind and body. In Turiya, one experiences the true nature of the self and the universe.

The Upanishads describe Turiya as follows:
1. The Fourth state, turiya, is neither inward nor outward-turned consciousness, nor the two together; not an undifferentiated mass of consciousness nor simple consciousness; not elusive nor grasping, without distinguishing, un-pierced by any ideas, activities, or perceptions; neither real nor unreal; not a concept; beyond the reach of mind and speech; tranquil; auspicious; non-dual. This is what is called the Fourth state, beyond cessation of the intellect (samadhi) and deep sleep. - Mandukya Upanishad
2. In the state of Turiya, the true nature of the self is revealed. The self is pure consciousness, beyond all limitations and du-

alities. It is the witness of all experiences and is unaffected by them. - Amritabindu Upanishad

3. In Turiya, one experiences the unity of the self and the universe. All distinctions and boundaries dissolve, and one realizes that everything is interconnected and inseparable. - Tejobindu Upanishad

4. Turiya is the state of supreme bliss and liberation. It is the goal of all spiritual practices and the ultimate realization of the self. - Mandukya Upanishad

Overall, Turiya is considered a state of supreme realization and transcendence. It is believed that through spiritual practice and meditation, one can attain this state and experience the true nature of the self and the universe.

There is a strong connection between Nada and Turiya, as both are considered to be states of higher consciousness that can be accessed through spiritual practice. The connection between Nada and Turiya is described in various Indian scriptures, such as the Yoga Sutras of Patanjali and the Hatha Yoga Pradipika.

In the Yoga Sutras, Patanjali describes Nada as the sound that can be heard through the practice of meditation, and he connects it with the state of Turiya:

Turiya is that state of pure consciousness which is beyond the range of perception of the senses, and which can be reached by the practice of Nada yoga. (Yoga Sutras 4.29)

Similarly, the Hatha Yoga Pradipika describes Nada as the inner sound that can be heard through the practice of Hatha yoga, and it connects it with the state of Turiya:

Through the practice of Hatha yoga, one can hear the inner sound (Nada), which leads to the state of Turiya, the fourth state of consciousness. (Hatha Yoga Pradipika 4.77)

Both scriptures suggest that through the practice of Nada yoga, one can access the state of Turiya, which is a state of pure consciousness beyond the range of perception of the senses.

Appendix

Reference Texts

Yoga Taravali of Adi Shankaracharya

I salute the lotus-feet of my guru that have experienced the knowledge and bliss of Atman, and that serve as a doctor for removing the delusion of people caused by the poison of samsara. (1)

In this world, there are 125,000 laya-yoga - the yoga of absorption in nature - meditations told by Lord Shiva. Of these, I consider the samadhi brought about by the meditation on the anahata sound to be the best. (2)

When by the rechaka, exhalation; puraka, inhalation; and kumbhaka, retention of air, all the nadis, channels for prana's flow, are purified, then knowledge rises of its own from the lotus of anahata chakra; this knowledge can only be known by oneself. (3)

O', meditation on the anahata sound, I salute you. I know that you are the ultimate goal among the laya-yogas. By your grace, my prana and mind get merged in the Lord's feet or the supreme state. (4)

The bandhakas, energy locks, of jalandhara, oddyana, and mula, have to be practised respectively, in the throat, stomach, and the base of the anus. If one knows and practises these three energy locks well, how can the cruel noose of time bind one? (5)

When the energy locks of oddyana, jalandhara, and mula awaken the coiled-up serpent woman, kundalini, then, the carrier of smell, air, moves downwards towards the sushumna nadi, and gives up its going out and coming in. (6)

By the constant compression of apana, the outward-moving energy, a flame of fire comes out of the muladhara chakra. This fire heats the moon of the sahasrara chakra and the other moons or centres of nadi in the body. Blessed in this world is the sadhaka, who drinks the nectar that flows from this heated moon. (7)

I do the one-pointed practice of kevala-kumbhaka that arises out of the practice of the three energy locks mentioned earlier. This kevala-kumbhaka is devoid of rechaka and puraka, and it removes the disturbance in the sense organs caused by their contact with sense objects. (8)

When the mind is fixed on the anahata chakra, then the actions of breathing and the mind are stopped. In this state, the splendour of kevala-kumbhaka is clearly seen. This splendor can be experienced by the alert and adept sadhakas. (9)

Though thousands of kumbhakas are mentioned in the hatha yoga texts, only the kevalakumbhaka has been acknowledged as the greatest, because in this greatest kumbhaka, prana's rechaka, also called prakrita; and prana's puraka, also called vainkrita; do not exist. (10)

When the calm inner space called trikuta becomes still by kevala-kumbhaka, then prana leaves the solar nadi, pingala;

and the lunar nadi, ida; and gets dissolved. (11)

The prana - which remains after it is consumed by the awakened kundalini- is controlled by kevala-kumbhaka, and leaves by the downward path, and gradually gets merged in the feet of the Lord or in the supreme state. (12)

Various restraints of the unchecked upward-motion of the breath are caused by kevalakumbhaka. This causes a dissolution of air in some wise yogis. Such dissolution is free from all disturbances of the senses. (13)

When raja yoga has properly developed, there is no need to focus upon goals; there is no need to control the mind; there is no need to observe the time and number of breath; there is no need to regulate the breath; and there is no need to put effort to attain concentration or meditation. (14)

Those who are established in raja yoga, are completely discarded by this manifested universe, and become one with Brahman. They have a strange state, without the states of waking and deep sleep; neither are they living nor dead. (15)

Those who have given up the ideas of 'I' and 'mine' and always have a calm mind and are established in the great raja yoga, they do not have the moods of the seer or the seen, and in that state, consciousness alone is manifested. (16)

Let the evolved state of mind, manonmani, be present in me, in which state, there is no opening or closing of the eyes, the exhalation or inhalation of air stops, and the mind also becomes free of resolves and choices. (17)

The inhaling and exhaling of breath stop because of prolonged restraint of the mind and the senses. In this state, the limbs of great yogis become immobile like the flame of a lamp in a windless place. The intellects of such yogis get merged in the evolved state of mind called manonmani. (18)

O' learned one! I tell you a method to attain the evolved state of mind, unmani: be indifferent to this universe and uproot all resolves with alertness. (19)

The mind that is constantly alerted to forcefully destroy the chain of resolves in the mind, becomes free of distractions and attachment to sense objects due to the destruction of the basis of all thoughts; and gradually attains peace. (20)

When there is a complete absence of breathing, immobility of the body, and the lotus of the eyes are in a half-open state, we see the manifestation of amanaska-mudra, the mindless-pose, in great sages. (21)

The great yogis, whose identification with the body has weakened because of spontaneously attaining the state of amanaska, attain a state beyond the mind that has no disturbances of the prana, and is infinite and limitless like the sky. (22)

When would I give up all the other states and attain that spontaneous state full of consciousness, which quietens all the senses and leads towards the union with the supreme Self? (23)

Due to excellent reflection on the indwelling Self, the previous attachments of persons go away and they attain a state of conscious sleep, yoga-nidra, which makes them give up all thoughts of this universe. (24)

By constant practice, the ever-benevolent yoga-nidra, appears in those yogis, whose resolves, choices, and the effects of actions have been completely uprooted. (25)

O' friend, getting convinced of and getting established in the state of turiya-which is beyond the three states of vishva, waking; taijasa, dreaming; and prajna, deep sleep-constantly experience the bliss of yoga-nidra that is full of consciousness, free from doubts, and inexplicable. (26)

Alas! When the sun of the supreme Self rises and the darkness of ignorance is completely dispelled, though the knowers of Self have a pure vision, they are unable to see anything in this entire universe. (27)

Staying in the cave of the Shrishailam mountain [a jyotirlinga temple of Shiva in Andhra Pradesh, India], when would I attain the perfection in samadhi that dissolves the mind, when creepers would entwine my body, and when birds would build their nests in my ears? (28)

When the prana becomes stable at the brahma-randhra, the anterior fontanelle, consciousness flows like the flow from the top of a mountain. One hears the anahata-sound, which is beyond the range of hearing, and there is no doubt that one gets mukti. (29)

Yoga Sikha Upanishad

Based on the translation by P. R. Ramachander

First Chapter

"All the living beings are surrounded by the net of illusion, Oh God, Parameshwara, Oh God of Gods, how will they attain salvation? Be kind enough to tell." Asked Lord Brahma to Lord Parameshwara and he replied as follows: 1.1

Some people say that the only way out is Jnana (knowledge). To attain occult powers, that alone will not suffice. How can Jnana without Yoga lead to salvation? It is also true that Yoga alone without Jnana will not lead to salvation. So, the one who aims at salvation, should learn Jnana and Yoga together. 1.2

Like a rope ties a bird, the minds of all living beings are tied. Enquiries and research do not affect the tie of this mind. So, the only way to win over this mind is through victory over Prana. There is no other option to get victory over Prana except Yoga and there are no methods except those shown by Siddhas. 1.3

So, I am teaching you this Yoga Shika (head of all yogas). It is greater than all Jnanas. After sitting in either Padmasana (lotus position) or any other Asana, and after concentrating the sight to the tip of the nose and after controlling both the hands and legs, meditate on the letter 'Om' with a concentrated mind.

If one continuously meditates on Parameshwara, he will become an expert in yoga and the Parameshwara would appear before him. 1.4

If we sit in an asana and continuously practice, the bindu will cease from going down. Without Pooraka and Rechaka, the Prana would stand in Kumbhaka for a very long time. You would hear different types of sound. The nectar will start flowing from the place of the moon. Hunger and thirst will cease. Mind would get concentrated on the ever-flowing bliss. The four steps for this are Mantra Yoga, Laya Yoga, Hatha Yoga and Raja Yoga. The great Maha Yoga, which is one, has been divided in to four and named as above.

The prana goes out with sound "ham" and goes in with the word "sa", and all beings naturally chant the mantra "Hamsa, Hamsa" (while exhaling and inhaling). This is chanted in the Sushumna after being taught by the Guru in an inverted manner (Hamsa inverted is soham). This chanting of the mantra "Soham, Soham (I am it)" is called Mantra Yoga. Sun is the letter "Ha" and moon is the letter "Tha".

The joining of sun and the moon is the Hatha Yoga. Due to Hatha Yoga, the idiocy which is the cause of all doshas (draw backs) is swallowed. When the merging of Jeevatma and Paramatma takes place, mind melts and vanishes. And only air of Prana remains. This is called Laya Yoga. Because of Laya Yoga that heavenly Swathmananda Sowkhya (the well-being of the joy of one's own soul) is attained. In the great temple of the middle of yoni (the female organ) the principle of the Devi, which is red like Hibiscus flower lives as Rajas in all beings.

The merger of this rajas with the male principle is called Raja Yoga. As a result of Raja Yoga, the Yogi gets all the occult powers like Anima. You have to understand that all these four types of Yogas are nothing but the merger of Prana, Apana and Samana. 1.5

For all those who have a body, their body is the temple of Shiva. It can give them occult powers. The triangular part in between the anus and penis is called the mooladhara. This is the place where Shiva lives as a life-giving force. There the Parashakthi called Kundalani lives.

From there wind is produced. Fire is also produced from there. From there only the sound 'Hamsa' and the mind are also produced. This place which would give whatever is asked for is called Kamakhya peetam (the seat of passion). In the edge of the anus is the Swadishtana Chakra with six petals. Near the belly is the Mani Poora Chakra with its ten petals. In the place near the heart the Anahatha Chakra with its 12 petals exists. And, Hey Lord Brahma, this is called the Poorna Giri Peeta. In the depression in the throat, Vishudhi Chakra with its 16 petals exists. Hey lord of Lords, that is Jalandara Chakra. In between the eyelids is the Agna Chakra with its two petals. Over that is the Maha Peeta called Udayana. 1.6

Second Chapter

This world functions because of the unclear foundation power which is described as Maha Maya, Maha Lakshmi, Maha Devi and Maha Saraswathi. That power shines in a micro form as a Bindu (dot) on the Peeta (seat). Bindu breaks the Peeta and emerges from there in the form of Nadha (sound). That Nadha Brahma assumes three shapes viz., Macro, Micro and external. The macro form is the big shape which is pervaded by the five Brahmans.

The micro form which arises from the Nadha with its three Bheejas (roots) is the form of Hiranya Garbha. Para is the ever-true property of Satchitananda. By continuously chanting the Atma mantra, the glitter will occur in Para Thathwa (the philosophy of the external). For the Yogi who has stopped his mind, this appears in the micro form similar to the flame of the lamp, moon's crescent, like a firefly, like a streak of lightning and like the glitter of stars.

There are no greater mantras than Nadha (sound), no Gods greater than Atma, no greater worship than the meditation and no pleasure greater than satisfaction. My devotee who understands this would remain stable in his happiness. To that great man who has great devotion to God as well as similar great devotion to his teacher, all this would be understood automatically.

Third Chapter

That great ever living Nadha (sound) is called Sabhda Brahman. It is the strength residing in the Mooladhara. Para is the foundation for its own self and is of the form of Bindhu. That Nadha coming out of Parashakthi (like the germ coming out of the seed) is called Pasyanthi (we see). The Yogis who can see using the Pasyanthi Shakthi, understand that it is the whole world. That power produces sound like rain starting from the heart. Hey Lord of Lords, there it is called Madhyama. It is called Vaikari when it merges in the sound form with Prana and exists in the throat and jaw. It produces all the alphabets from Aa to Ksha. From alphabet words arise and from words rise the sentences and from them all the Vedas and Mantras. This Goddess Saraswathi lives in the cave of intelligence in all beings. In meditation when will power melts, you can reach this Para Thathwa.

Fourth Chapter

Because the divine power is single, there are no differences there. You must understand that the thought process of living beings is like seeing a snake in a rope. When you do not know, it is a rope and then for a small time the rope appears as a snake. Ordinary intelligence is similar to this. We see everything as the world that we see. There is no reason or basis for this world to be different from this Brahman. So the World is only Brahman and not anything different. If you understand the Para Thathwa like this, where is the cause for differentiation. 4.1

In Taittiriya Upanishad fear has been told as belonging to that foolish person who finds difference between Jeevatma (soul) and Paramatma (God). Though this world has been said as something to be experienced, in the next moment it vanishes like a dream. There is no state of waking up in a dream. There is no dream in the state of waking up. Neither are there in Laya. Laya is not in both. All these three are illusions created by the three characters. The one who sees this would be above characteristics and would be forever. 4.2

The Chaithanya (activity) starts in the form of the world. All these are Brahman. It is useless to differentiate it as Atma and Anatma when dealing with wise people. The foolish man thinks that body is attached to the soul. The belief that a pot is mixed with the mud and the water is mixed with mirage and similarly the belief that body is mixed up with the soul is because of taking recourse to ignorance. 4.3

Fifth Chapter

That Yogi who has mastered yoga and who has complete control over his senses would attain whatever he imagines. The Teacher (guru) is Brahma, He is Vishnu and He is the Lord of Lords Sadashiva and there is nobody greater than the teacher in all the three worlds. We should worship with devotion Parameshwara, who is the great Soul who has taught us divine knowledge. The one who worships like that would get the result of Jnana fully. Do not keep your aim because of the wavering mind on occult powers. The one who knows this principle well is the one who has attained salvation. There is no doubt about it.

Sixth Chapter

That great light in which the Bhoo Loka, Bhuvar Loka and Suvar Loka [Worlds] and the Sun, Moon, and Fire Gods, are but a small part in the letter "Om". When the mind wavers, worldly life and when it is firm, salvation will result. So, Lord

Brahma, using great intelligence we must keep the mind not to waver. For desire to possess wealth, the mind is the reason. When that is destroyed, the world would be destroyed. One should, with a lot of effort, start the treatment for that. When a man looks after his mind using his mind and realizes that it has stopped running, he would see the Parabrahman, which is very difficult to see. The Yogi can get salvation by seeing his mind with his mind. We must see the mind with the mind and hanker for that mad state. We must see the mind with the mind and be stable in Yoga. 6.1

In any place where the wind moves, the mind also wavers. The mind is called moon, sun, wind, sight and fire. The Bindu (dot), Nadha (sound) and the Kala (crescent) are the Gods Vishnu, Brahma, and Ishwara. By constant practice of Nadha, the bad influences will vanish. That which is Nadha becomes the Bindu and then becomes the mind. One must clearly aim at the unification of Nadha, Bindu and Chintha. The mind itself is the Bindu and that is the reason for the state of creation of the world. Like milk being produced by the cow, Bindu is produced by the mind. 6.2

The one who realizes well the six wheels (Agna chakras) enters the world of pleasure. One must enter it by controlling the air in the body. One must send the air (Vayu) upwards. One must practice Vayu, Bindu Chakra and Chintha. Once the Yogi realizes Samadhi by one of them, he feels that everything is nectar like. Like the fact that the fire inside the wood cannot be brought out without churning it by another wood, without practice, the lamp of wisdom cannot be lit. Adopting his teacher as the one who pilots the ship and by adopting his teachings as the stable ship, with the power of constant practice, one crosses the sea of this birth. Thus tells this Upanishad.

The Fourth State of Consciousness

Turiya is beyond all mortal strife,
Mind is stilled, and consciousness unveiled,
Self is seen, as pure and boundless life,
Lose all limits - all illusions have failed.

No waking dream, no deep sleep's veil,
Does touch the state of Turiya's pure light,
Where all is one, and all is without fail,
So, all distinctions vanish from our sight.

In Nada's realm, beyond all space and time,
Self is free - all is pure and still,
What need for thought, no need for reason's mime,
For all is known, and all is pure and real.

Oh Turiya, the Nada's state of soul,
Let us find the peace that makes us whole.

More Books by Rudra Shivananda

Chakra selfHealing by the Power of Om

Yoga of Purification and Transformation

Surya Yoga - Healing by Solar Power

Breathe Like Your Life Depends On It

In Light of Kriya Yoga

Healing Postures of the 18 Siddhas

Insight and Guidance for Spiritual Seekers

Practical Mantra Yoga

Breathe Better Live Longer

Living A Spiritual Life In A Material World

The Bhagavad Gita Reference Guide

Transformed by The Presence

Howling From The High Heavens

website: www.rudrashivananda.com
blog: www.sanatanamitra.com
www.youtube.com/user/KriyaNathYogi

About the Author

Rudra Shivananda, a disciple of the Himalayan GrandMaster Yogiraj Gurunath Siddhanath, is dedicated to the service of humanity through the furthering of human awareness and spiritual evolution. He teaches that the only lasting way to bring happiness into one's life is by a consistent practice of awareness and transformation. He has developed healing programs utilizing the energy centers [Chakras] and Prana Energy techniques through breath.

Rudra Shivananda is committed to spreading the message of his Master: "Earth Peace through Self Peace". He teaches this message of World and Individual Peace through the practice of Kriya Yoga. As a student and teacher of yoga for more than 50 years, he is trained as an Acharya or Spiritual Preceptor in the Indian Nath Tradition, closely associated with the Siddha tradition. He lives in the San Francisco Bay area, and has given initiations and workshops in USA, Ireland, England, Japan, Spain, Brazil, Russia, Singapore, Malaysia, Hong Kong, India, Australia, Canada and Estonia.